PILGRIM'S GUIDE
TO THE
NEW AGE
ALICE & STEPHEN LAWHEAD

A LION BOOK
Tring · Batavia · Sydney

Copyright © 1986 Alice and Steve Lawhead

Published by
Lion Publishing Corporation
1705 Hubbard Avenue, Batavia, Illinois 60510, USA
ISBN 0 85648 944 1
Lion Publishing plc
Icknield Way, Tring, Herts, England
ISBN 0 85648 944 1
Albatross Books Pty Ltd
PO Box 320, Sutherland, NSW 2232, Australia
ISBN 0 86760 813 7

First edition 1986
British Library Cataloguing in Publication Data

Lawhead, Stephen
　　Pilgrim's guide to the new age.
　　1. Sociology, Christian　2. Social history
　　——— 1970—
　　I. Title　　　II. Lawhead, Alice
　　261.8′3　　　BT738
　　ISBN 0-85648-944-1

Printed in Italy

Photographs in this book are reproduced by permission of the
following photographers and agencies:

Andes Press Agency/Carlos Reys 103
Architectural Association 23, 32, 75
Eric Auerbach 81 (below)
Barnaby's Picture Library 30 (above left and below), 32 (above),
　　56 (above and below), 58, 65
Robin Bath 69
BBC Hulton 25, 72, 85/UPI-Bettmann Archive 76
BBDO (UK) 91
BPCC/Aldus Archive 16, 17 (below), 61 (all), 93, 95
　　96 (both)/Illustrated London News — Major Plunkett 97
British Antarctic Survey/B. Tearle 4
Richard Bryant 70–71
Paul Craven 35, 36, 88
DACS 1986 78 (above and below)
Mary Evans Picture Library 8 (below), 22, 25 (Thoreau, Lincoln,
　　Beethoven), 38, 42 (above), 60, 89 (right)
Sonia Halliday Photographs/FHC Birch 3, cover (clouds), rainbow
　　running head
　　/Sister Daniel running head tour three
　　/Sonia Halliday 107, 108, running head tour one
　　/Laura Lushington running head tours four and six
　　/Else Trickett running head tour seven
Lion Publishing/Jon Willcocks 54 (below), 74, 86, running head
　　tour five
Mansell Collection 13 (left)
NASA 102
National Film Archive 25 (above)
Natural History Photographic Agency 106
Pictorial Press 104 (inset)
Picturebank 46–47
Popperfoto 31, 89 (left)
Jean-Luc Ray 38 (right)
Rex Features 17 (above), 80, 83 (all)
Mick Rock/Cephas Picture Library 49, 67
Science Photo Library 7, P.A. McTurk and D. Parker/14–15,
　　US Navy/19, Douglas W. Johnson/58, Hank Morgan/59, J.
　　Stevenson/87, Mazziotta
Select/Julian Simmonds 48, 52, 54 (above), 66
Doug Sewell 99
Clifford Shirley 40
David Simson 39 (left), 43, 45, 57
Leonard Smith 110–11
Spectrum 37 (left and below left), 51
Peter Stiles 1, 32 (below), 101 and cover
Topham 8 (above), 13 (Galileo, Darwin, Einstein), 30
　　(above right), 53, 55, 63, 73, 81 (above), 104–5
David Townsend 33
John Williams Studio 4, 20, 34, 50, 68, 84, 100 (below), 112
ZEFA (UK) 5, 6, 10–11, 12, 21, 26–27, 37 (right), 38 (left),
　　39 (right), 42 (below right)

Contents

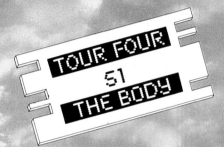

What is the New Age, and can I get there from here?

Do they accept Travelers Checks?

Should I bring sensible shoes?

If you're one of the few billion people who, from time to time, ask yourself these questions, this book is for you.

Whether you realize it or not, you are proceeding on a journey through the New Age. Our opinion is that you might as well go First Class. This invaluable *Pilgrim's Guide* will point out the dead ends, detours, hazardous routes, falling rocks and shortcuts through this often strange, always fascinating place.

Is this trip necessary?

It's more than that. It's inevitable. Everyone must journey through the New Age.

Can I take my body with me?

Of course, many people do. Others prefer to travel light. We agree that baggage should be kept to an absolute minimum. Actually, your only real necessity will be an open mind. (The people at *Pilgrim's Guide* cannot provide you with an open mind. Each traveler must provide his or her own, and must have it ready before the tour begins.)

Will I be safe?

What if I get lost?

The New Age is not usually a dangerous place, but it can be very confusing. Many travelers wander aimlessly their entire lives. A few cautious souls refuse to venture from the hotel lobby, fearing loss of direction or worse. But that's where we come in. *Pilgrim's Guide to the New Age* can take the worry out of wandering. This practical book makes getting lost in the New Age a thing of the past.

We at *Pilgrim's Guide* are in the business of conducting travelers like yourself on journeys of discovery. We have the credentials, we have the experience, we have the know-how. Say no more.

When do we leave?

Immediately. So, sit back, relax, enjoy the view, and leave the driving to us. We haven't lost a pilgrim yet.

Bon Voyage!

TOUR ONE

TAKE ONE HUMAN

THE COSMOS

BIG, AND GETTING BIGGER

Most pilgrims have a hazy idea that the Cosmos — *everything* that exists in any way, shape or form, including but not limited to what we call our own universe — is merely a few billion assorted stars along with the odd galaxy or two floating in a rather chilly void.

For some time, however, a quiet revolution has been going on in the cosmic surveying business. And as more and more answers wash ashore from the oceans of computer-generated data, it appears that the scale of the universe is something quite radically large in the extreme. Seriously huge. A place to get really lost in.

For example, if you decided to trek from one side of the Milky Way galaxy to the other — just to have something to do — and if you started out on a good day, traveling at the speed of light (which hardly anyone

does), your journey would take 600,000 years to complete. (We recommend bringing along a nice longish novel to read. *War and Peace*, perhaps.)

On your trip, you would encounter many of the Milky Way's 100 billion stars, which come in a generous selection of shades and sizes from Red Giant to White Dwarf. That figure is actually a rough estimate, of course. No one, to date, has actually applied him or herself to the task of counting each and every star. At the rate of one per second, it would take slightly more than three hundred years to get the job done, and that's simply more time than most people are willing to devote to the project.

And, having completed such a count of stars in the Milky Way, there's the matter of logging the stars in the other (estimated) 100 billion galaxies in the universe.

The quest for a more complete understanding of this vast universe has, interestingly enough, brought scientists to a renewed interest in the

'The most incomprehensible thing about the world is that it is incomprehensible.'
Albert Einstein

The Andromeda Galaxy is the nearest neighbour in space to our own galaxy – and yet it is 1,467,000 light years distant. The amount of empty space in the Universe is equivalent to an empty twenty-mile cube containing a single grain of sand.

atom. In order to study the largest thing known to the human race, it has become necessary to study the smallest. In other words, if you hope to explain a Black Hole, you must first understand sub-atomic inter-actions. The two are related in no uncertain terms.

Those who have trouble grasping the enormity of the macrocosm will take small comfort from the fact that the microcosm is at least as small as the universe is large, and indeed appears to be getting smaller. The atom (once thought to be the smallest divisible parcel of raw matter) can be sub-divided into yet smaller constituents: neutrons, protons and electrons — electrons being the smallest. The latest finding is that these same smaller parcels which make up the atom can be broken down even further into quarks.

Quarks are the gnomes of science: playful, mischievous, invisible, difficult to catch. By unraveling the mystery of quarks and their cousins — leptons, muons, and tauons —

physicists hope to get a firmer grasp on the universe, since the behavior of the tiny quark directly impacts the behavior of nearly everything else in the universe, no matter how big or far away.

New Age dwellers spend a lot of time thinking about the cosmos, about the universe and their place in it. They like to examine it, form theories about it, and fly around it in little space capsules. For there is a hope that in explaining the cosmos we can explain ourselves: who we are, where we came from, where we're going.

And with a little bit of luck we might even find the answer to the biggest questions: Why? and How?

At 71,500 times its actual size, this strand of DNA has had a single gene mapped out in blue. DNA, which contains the basic genetic information for life, was only discovered in the 1950s.

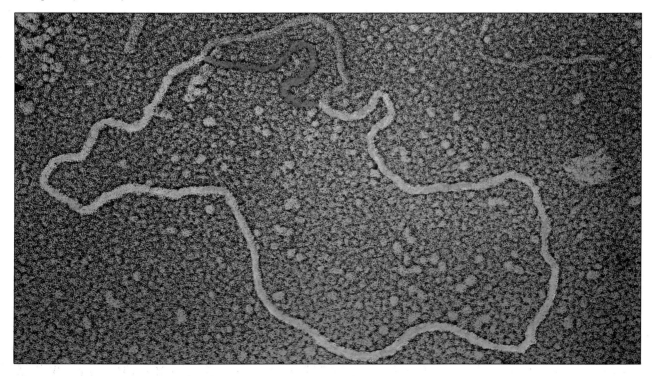

Albert Einstein, demonstrating relatively bad manners.

E=MC² AND ALL THAT

The attentive pilgrim will have noticed by now that the New Age is an exceedingly relative place. In fact, *relative* may be *the key word* for the New Age — a word which took on cosmic significance in 1905 when an unknown Swiss patent clerk published a modest little scientific paper.

Tame as beginnings go, both the paper and the clerk might easily have been forgotten if not for the fact that the clerk was Albert Einstein and the paper his 'Special Theory of Relativity'.'

STAR GAZING

It's a confusing world out there, and in ancient times (around 2,000 BC, especially in and around Babylonia) people tried to make some sense of the universe by looking up. Heavenly bodies, they found, were remarkably constant, and reassuringly organized. The sun, moon and stars were, by earthly standards, so reliable that they formed the basis of time measurement.

Most of the stars hung suspended in the sky, stable and predictable, revolving in slow, stately orbits around the earth — or so it seemed to the ancients. A few, however, had the ability to wander at will throughout the cosmos. They must be gods! They were given god-names: Venus, Mercury, Jupiter, Mars and the rest.

Upon further study, it appeared that the stars whimsically formed themselves into the skeletons of animals, people and objects. Taurus, the bull; Gemini, the twins; the Big Dipper. But that wasn't all. As the ancient astronomers looked at the stars, and as they observed events in their own lives, they noted a synchronicity between events in the heavens and events on earth. They began studying how the two related, and astrology was born.

The prophecies of Nostradamus (published around 1555) were based, for the most part, on astrological projections. Many people in those days set great store by Nostradamus — and many still do.

Nostradamus: prophecies to set your watch by?

But astrology came upon hard times when the scientific age emerged. The stars no longer held the key to understanding; science did. It was not the stars that caused storms or plagues; it was atmospheric conditions or bacteria that could be explained easily with the theories and tools of modern science. The prevailing belief that long journeys, marriages, family affairs, finances, and health succeeded or failed because of astrological conditions fell by the wayside. In 1898, the *Larousse Encyclopedia* stated: 'Astrology has hardly any adherents other than swindlers who play on public credulity, and even these are fast disappearing.' Most people didn't know the sign under which they were born. Who cared?

And then, after World War 1, newspapers hungry for back-page filler copy began to publish modest horoscopes for their readers. Nothing fancy, just entertaining little squibs: 'Renew a friendship today; you will be lucky in business this week.'

The pithy predictions were irresistible. The horoscopes came to be widely read, and were great circulation-builders. No one took them seriously, but it was amusing every morning to read what the day would bring. And you know, sometimes the horoscopes really were right! They said it would be a day full of promise, and, by golly, it was! This sparked an interest in more complete, more individualized horoscopes, which the neo-astrologers were more than happy to provide.

Astrology — the belief that heavenly bodies have a direct effect on mundane human affairs — experienced a renaissance. Its practice has become part and parcel of the New Age belief that human affairs are inextricably bound up with the forces of the physical universe. Bring on The Age of Aquarius.

Working with mathematical formulas, Albert Einstein theorized that ordinary, everyday sunlight did not follow the regularly accepted laws of motion established by Sir Isaac Newton. In fact, Einstein insisted, light behaved according to its own quirky rules, and was inextricably bound up with such distantly related things as mass, energy, speed and time.

Unassuming as all this might sound, this little paper revolutionized the universe overnight and almost nothing has been the same since. For tucked away in the neat calculations was the potent notion that the universe observed via the human senses was

---

Just when $E=mc^2$ was starting to make sense, along comes quantum mechanics to give you a run for your money. Quantum mechanics is to sub-atomic particles what general relativity is to galaxies — one deals with quarks and the other with quasars.

The Holy Grail of New Age physics is the Grand Unifying Theory — GUT, as it is playfully called. The idea is that a theory lurks out there in the dim unknown, a theory that will explain everything. That is, *Everything*: light, gravity, space, time, electromagnetism, energy, matter. The GUT (or GUTs — there are probably more than one) will not only explain all these diverse entities but wrap them neatly and tie them with a bow.

The elusive GUT concerns a very basic, yet-to-be-discovered, force of nature physicists call the *superforce*. It's the force that not only encompasses all known forces (gravity, electromagnetism, what have you), but enables the creation of the universe itself out of absolutely nothing. Once we've got our finger on the superforce, we'll be able to recreate creation, literally, or at least manipulate the cosmos to our liking, because the superforce is responsible for generating all known forces and all physical structures. The superforce is the very wellspring of all existence.

MAY THE SUPERFORCE BE WITH YOU

Theorists speculate that once upon a time the superforce created space, created matter, nudged the forces we see today into being, and thereby shaped our universe. (Sounds suspiciously like God, doesn't it?)

In harnessing the superforce, we'll be able to shape space, control time, and suspend gravity or vice versa. We'll make matter to order, thus creating our own exotic worlds with bizarre properties. With the superforce in hand, we'll strip away the many dimensions of space like the layers of an onion, and run time sideways if it suits us. In the words of physicist Paul Davies, 'Truly, we should be lords of the universe.'

All this is not idle speculation, mind you, or the musing of trance-happy mystics. These ideas come from respected, Nobel Prize-winning scientists and are based on sound scientific principles. In fact, several breakthroughs have been made recently in GUT research. Nuclear physicists have managed to unify two of the universe's fundamental forces and the race is now on to unify the others into a Super-GUT.

By now you're probably asking yourself, 'Who, save someone with three PhDs in astrophysics, cares about any of this?'

Everyone who believes in God as Creator of the Universe cares. To them, this all seems as though science has come full circle and is now willing to admit that there is a unifying force in the universe, an overriding presence that can explain the workings of the cosmos for the simple reason that He/She/It created the cosmos.

Christians are especially interested — and even a little smug. After centuries of taking a beating from Copernicus, Galileo, Darwin and a host of scientists whose findings and theories have seemed to place traditional Christian thought about the creation of the universe in a rather dim light, they are now leaning back, putting their feet up on the desk, and clicking their tongues as if to say, 'We knew that if you studied long enough, and hard enough, and gave this whole business some serious thought . . . you'd find the truth.'

The *Guide* would have you understand that whether you know it or not, our world is being shaped by these esoteric ideas in one way or another — if not physically (yet), then at least psychologically. The hard sciences (mathematics, chemistry, physics), and the soft sciences (philosophy, psychology, theology) are melting, merging, and forming strange new amalgamations.

Increasingly, mathematicians talk like mystics, and scientific journals read like holy writ. Physics is becoming indistinguishable from metaphysics. Scientists trained in the rigorous scientific methods, graduates of the school of naturalism, have pushed that naturalism to its furthest extreme — to the extent that the most unlikely people have become *super*naturalists. New Age travelers should be aware of this quiet revolution so that they do not become unduly confused when accosted by physicists wearing clerical robes, chanting formulaic mantras.

This ancient stone circle at Castlerigg in Cumberland is one of many that stand in the British Isles. New Agers have seen them as landing markers for extraterrestial spacecraft, or as accumulators of ancient magic power. But all that can be safely said is that they were used to study the stars and in religious rituals.

not necessarily the universe as it really, truly existed.

The idea startled the world. For if such age-old, rock-solid absolutes as the movement and behavior of time could be proven mere relativities, what next?

It was not long before the relativity of the physical universe became linked up with relativity in the moral universe, as certain people, no doubt looking for just this sort of philosophical justification, smuggled the heart of the theory into the moral realm and transplanted it there — much to Einstein's horror.

The theory became the catalyst that set in motion a chain-reaction of thought that went something like this:

Since one's description of the universe depends on where one sits to look at it, who's to say which description is right? If all descriptions are relative to a personal point of view, there is no absolutely right way of looking at things. Therefore there is no right or wrong, only points of view. Hence, any point of view is right.

The moral universe became just as relative as the physical universe, and

age-old absolutes fell one by one to the inexorable gravity of the idea. No longer were such things as murder and theft immutable ethical laws — they could be, in certain circumstances, changed to fit the situation. Truth, in other words, could be made to serve circumstance.

Thus truth itself was shown to be relative, for if it served circumstance it could change as circumstances changed. If truth depended on where one stood to look at it, what then could be the measuring stick for human affairs? People searched for a substitute and came up with *sincerity*.

An idea or action or course of behavior could be considered moral if the originator was sincere. No other measure need be applied. What other measure was there? All that was required was that one really, sincerely believe in what one was saying or doing and who could question it? Since all points of view were equally valid, if one sincerely believed oneself to be right, ethical truth was thereby established.

Truth has to do with veracity,

integrity and honesty, and is therefore not open to personal point of view. Sincerity, on the other hand, deals only with genuineness, which is much more subjective and therefore infinitely more malleable. Truth, with its stern visage, was replaced by sincerity, with its ambiguous smirk, and the moral universe was rocked to the core.

LOST IN SPACE

Your *Guide* warned you at the start that the New Age can be confusing. But no, contrary to all appearances, we're not off course. We just took a detour. We had to take a brief look at the panorama of New Age ideas about the cosmos.

There are, as you can see, numerous theories about the universe, and where humans fit into everything. This is nothing new — there have always been theories about this.

Take Ptolemy, for example. He was the Greek astronomer/geographer who figured out that the earth is central to the universe, with all the stars and planets revolving around

it. This may seem absurd, but it was the accepted explanation for over 1,300 years. It matched with the observations of generations of star-gazers, and it supported their belief that mankind was the focal point of all creation.

Then, in the 1500s, Copernicus started to observe things a little differently. He published a book that stated that the planets orbitted the sun, not the earth. When Copernicus and, later, Galileo, claimed that the earth wasn't geographically central to the universe, it made a great many people angry. It suggested an unsettling corollary: that man wasn't the existential focus of creation, either.

'Heresy!' they told Galileo. 'Lies and heresy!' It was a dangerous time to be a heretic, as you might remember. There was an Inquisition going on, and under threat of torture, excommunication and worse, Galileo was forced to recant, and his research was forbidden to be published. It

ANCIENT ASTRONAUTS

One popular adjunct to UFOlogy is the ancient astronaut concept. Simply stated, the theory proposes that back in human civilization's infancy, Earth was visited by highly advanced aliens. How else can one explain the pyramids? Or mythology? Or the national debt?

Through several wide-eyed books, Erich von Daniken has pursued this theory into general parlance. Were it not for his own infectious enthusiasm the notion probably would have died on the vine. Instead, his books *Chariots of the Gods?*, *Gods from Outerspace*, *Gold of the Gods*, and *In Search of Ancient Gods* have made believers of millions. Not to mention making millions for believer von Daniken.

(The *Guide* has learned that the soon-to-be-released *Luxury Yachts of the Gods* offers a startling new perspective on ancient mariners.)

That there *are* fairly reasonable explanations to most of the mysteries von Daniken poses does not deter ancient astronaut buffs in the least.

MIND-AT-LARGE

Several of you asked when we began if you would need your body for your journey through the New Age. Not if you're into psychic travel, Silva Mind Control, or any other number of beliefs that assert the absolute reality of a universe beyond — an invisible universe next door to the visible universe we all know. This invisible universe exists beyond the scope and dimensions of our own normal, everyday universe, which we can explore with our physical senses. Though we may not be able to see, hear, smell or touch this other universe, we can take up residence there, if we only put our minds to it.

Therefore, each human being is, potentially, Mind-at-Large. Mind-at-Large means that the multi-dimensional universe is your oyster. You can be absolutely anywhere at any time (or even everywhere all the time) — whatever 'where' and 'time' mean.

Astrology maintains that our lives are influenced by stellar activity in the heavens. But believers in Mind-at-Large claim the opposite — that the stars are influenced by human activity.

When in tune with Mind-at-Large, time and space are elastic. Time goes forward and backward; space can turn itself inside out. Thoughts travel at will, unhindered and unaffected by physical laws of any kind.

Mind-at-Large has been called other things by other people:

'A separate reality' (Castaneda)

'Clairvoyant reality' (LeShan)

'Other spaces' (Lilly)

'Other realities' (Leonard)

'Another order of reality' (Brodie)

'Supermind' (Rosenfeld)

You get the idea. Leave your body behind and journey through the cosmos, exploring at will a parallel universe where literally anything can happen.

wasn't a good idea to even talk about Galileo in those days. So much for the 16th century's response to scientific thinking.

Eventually, though, the evidence for a planetary system revolving around the sun — a solar system — became undeniable, and humankind had to reconcile itself to the fact that the world didn't revolve around it. In time, people adjusted to this and went on to find other reasons to believe that humankind, although not physically central to the universe, was certainly the mental, spiritual, moral and existential pivot.

All went along smoothly in this area — until Charles Darwin. Darwin observed nature and its mysterious ways and advanced the theory that human beings were merely the most fully developed animal on Earth — the last link at the top end of a long interconnected chain of creatures. He theorized that humans were evolved from apes, who were evolved from monkeys, who were in turn evolved from lower forms of life.

The outcry was horrendous. 'Apes! Never! Mankind is God's unique creation! He has an immortal soul! Read your Bible, man!'

Here was yet another science-induced heresy, voiced without respect to prevailing religious belief, not to mention the traditional six-day creation account in the Jewish and Christian Bible. For some people, though, Darwin's theories were extremely attractive. They provided a reasonable explanation for some previously inscrutable phenomena.

A hundred years later, the jury is still out on much of Darwin's evolutionary theory, and while it is the generally accepted blueprint for how life came into existence on this planet, crucial 'links' between sub-human and human life have yet to be found. And now, the old evolutionary theory is being modified by more advanced theories presenting a sort of spontaneous origination of several basic kinds of animals, mutation and other new speculations.

The important thing about Darwin, as it relates to this question of where humans sit at the cosmic banquet, is that Darwin upset everyone's idea of what was absolute. People were feeling pretty comfortable with the idea that man was number one in the universe (so comfortable they didn't give a thought to the possibility that he might *not* be) and then along came Darwin, suggesting that we are all merely clever apes without the fur coat.

From the left: Copernicus, Galileo, Darwin and Einstein. Each of them turned the ideas of the day on their heads, and changed the way we see and understand the world.

'The sun, the moon, and the stars would have disappeared long ago, had they happened to be within reach of predatory human hands.'
Havelock Ellis

PARASITES ON THE PLANET

Then the world began to change in strange, frightening ways.

The planet started showing signs of wear. Rivers were drying up; air over many cities grew noxious, unbreatheable, the water undrinkable. The soil began losing its natural ability to produce. Vast open areas of the planet became overcrowded and diseased. Polluted rivers caught fire. Even vast oceans became foul.

Commercial industrialization — the once-bright hope of the modern world — spawned factories and working conditions that bred illness, injury, exploitation of the workforce, and in many cases revolution.

Adolph Hitler and his élite band of thugs went on a murderous rampage, killing millions of Jews, Catholics, and miscellaneous 'undesirables,' and plunged the whole world into a bloody, devastating war.

In 1944, the United States flattened the Japanese cities of Hiroshima and Nagasaki by dropping on them the latest in their technological arsenal — the atom bomb. The damage — immediate and long range — staggered the collective imagination of the entire world.

What to make of all this? Of course, all along there had been those who suspected that man was an obnoxious guest, imposing rather ruthlessly on the gracious hospitality of the universe.

Pollution, exploitation for profit, Nazism, destruction, and the dreadful power of nuclear weapons combined to offer proof for a once-obscure belief: man was, at heart, an animal with a brain too big for his own good. Man as 'a wise fool' became a popular characterization of the human race.

'Man may be the most developed, the most intelligent, the most gifted, and the most "supreme" of all life forms on this planet, but he is obviously a moral moron, a negligent and reckless caretaker of the world's resources.' Humankind began to emerge in popular thought as a destroyer rather than a creator, an incompetent manager of the resources entrusted to him.

As a result, a few people decided that unless something changed in human nature, all of our problems would soon be solved by default, because the earth simply would not take much more abuse. The time had come once again to redefine our place in the universe, to put the human race in perspective — just as it was done in Copernicus' and Galileo's and Darwin's day.

The twentieth century presents the human race with an ultimatum. Man must be transformed into a different kind of creature or else he will perish, and the rest of the universe will perish with him. Like the phoenix of ancient myth, he must somehow rise from the ashes of Hiroshima, Dachau and Ethiopia, emerge from the disasters and death of the past and present, and be reborn into an inspired existence where all technology is developed and used with respect to moral and human concerns; where the environment is treated with respect, as one would a beloved friend; where cruelty towards those of the same species is no longer practiced.

Nice idea — but will it work?

'Hitherto man had to live with the idea of death as an individual; from now onward, mankind will have to live with the idea of its death as a species.'
Arthur Koestler

'The modern choice is between non-violence or non-existence.'
Martin Luther King Jr.

IS ANYBODY OUT THERE?

'Isn't it a bit egocentric,' ask some, 'to assume that in this huge universe, in this endless cosmos, our little planet — which is only one among countless billions — is the only one inhabited by intelligent life? If nothing else, aren't the odds against such a view?'

And indeed, the argument that we have space brothers, not to mention space sisters, is tantalizing if not convincing. Numerous reported sightings — most of them since 1950 — add fuel to the flame, and the possibility of visits from other planets is taken seriously by such august groups as the United States Air Force, NASA, the CIA, the RAF, and governments around the world.

Unidentified flying objects. Flying saucers. Those brightly glowing fireballs that well-heeled alien visitors from outer-space whiz around in. While humans have always been fascinated with the heavens, and have always seen in it strange, unexplained things, the belief is emerging that those same strange, unexplained things are UFOs — space ships sent by alien intelligences to a) explore, b) save, c) conquer, d) bamboozle our planet.

UFOlogists believe that UFOs and their occupants are here on serious business of one type or another, either as 'angels' (a benign invasion) or 'devils' (calamity). Some branches of UFOlogy preach that the Earth was visited long ages ago and 'seeded' by superior spacemen, our primeval ancestors, who may or may not be coming back again. Others believe that UFO contact represents an attempt on the part of

benevolent space brothers to steer our civilization towards higher enlightenment.

With its things-that-go-bump-in-the-night brand of spookiness and a limited amount of the kind of hard data scientists demand, UFOlogy has generally remained the dominion of cranks and hoaxers. Poorly verified reports of sightings and contacts, and a few fuzzy photographs have provoked interest, but in most cases are hardly enough to make believers out of the scientific community in general.

Recently, however, serious scientists have become taken with the idea of life in outer space. No-nonsense men like Carl Sagan and Frank Drake suggest that, on the basis of statistics alone, there ought to be billions and billions of earth-type planets out there capable of supporting intelligent life, and even if only a tiny fraction of these planets are peopled, that still works out to millions and millions of inhabited planets. Out of all those millions of inhabited

Two veteran UFO-spotters scan the skies near Warminster in England. Extraterrestials seem to prefer Warminster, as their vehicles are so often reported to be seen there.

planets, surely one or two civilizations would be more advanced than we are in circumnavigating deep space. Therefore, it makes good statistical sense to believe that our space brothers are out there somewhere watching and waiting, or perhaps on their way with the Welcome Wagon.

This notion has been taken seriously enough in scientific circles to warrant a solid scientific acronym: SETI (the Search for Extra-Terrestrial Intelligence). One manifestation of SETI was realized when the satellite Pioneer 10 took off in 1972, carrying a little gold plaque bearing a male and female likeness, and a map showing how to find Earth — a greeting card to anyone out there who might intercept the satellite.

That gold greeting card was only a trifle, however, when you compare the time, effort and money that has gone into constructing gigantic radio telescopes around the world. These enormous devices are regularly put to the task of scanning the heavens for radio signals from outer space in the hope that alien civilizations are as interested as we are in getting together, and are beaming messages of goodwill in our general direction. Scientists make routine attempts to send messages as well, although the chances of ever knowing whether or not a message has been received is depressingly slim.

Some investigators, however, insist that the lack of objective evidence is not all that surprising if you take the point of view that UFOs are actually a *subjective* phenomenon. That is, an event that takes place wholly (or in large part) in the mind of the beholder. UFOs might be 'projections' of some kind, produced for some effect, by an entity or entities unknown. This answers a number of questions, but not all. Ultimately, we're left back at square one: Who is behind this? What's it all about?

Be it chariots of the gods, or alien jokes that have fallen decidedly flat, UFOlogists assert that we are not alone in the universe. We have company and had better learn to be a bit more hospitable if we ever hope to be invited to the Great Galactic Fancy Dress Ball.

HUMAN BEINGS, GOOD OR BAD?

Our optimism concerning the ability (or inability) of the human race to be transformed will depend on what we believe about the nature of human beings.

We all have our ideas about this, and they may change on a daily basis, depending on how we happen to perceive our fellow human beings at any given moment. Were the kids adorable or mischievous today? Was the world news encouraging or discouraging? Was the salesperson polite or rude?

The struggle to understand human nature has been a continuing quest for Christians. Even with almost 2,000 years of tradition to fall back on, Christians continue to question human nature, the affability of the universe, and the place of human-kind in the general scheme of things. In this way, then, Christians plug in quite naturally to the mood of the New Age. They are, in their better moments, open to new ideas,

experiences, and philosophies — while still firmly believing that God rules over the whole Universe, and that Jesus is God's Son. They believe that a transformation of the human spirit is desperately needed.

Each of the two popular possibilities that our society entertains — humans basically good or humans basically bad — have, in the past 2,000 years, had their champions and detractors. The options are . . .

The American MX missile represents a new breed in nuclear weaponry. The 'overkill' rate (the number of times existing weapons could destroy the human race) is now so high as to be horrifyingly meaningless.

Astrology isn't the only New Age belief or practice that comes to us direct from the ancient world. The idea that the universe is chock full of spiritual beings, and that these beings form a hierarchy at whose head stands the Sky God, is old — decidedly old.

The Sky God (according to New Age animists, pantheists, and neo-pagans) is not a creator-God, but merely the most highly developed of the innumerable spirits inhabiting the universe.

These spirits are believed to possess varying temperaments: some are cruel and capricious, others are friendly and fun-loving. If we are going to get along

ANIMALS, VEGETABLES, MINERALS

in the universe, we had better learn how to please the nice spirits (through gifts, offerings, ceremonies and incantations), and to placate the nasty ones — or, better yet, to steer entirely clear of them.

Witches, sorcerers, shamans and warlocks, it is said, understand and know how to control the spirits. Ordinary folks should look to the local shaman or witch for help and guidance when confronted with illness, drought and sudden reversals of fortune. These intercessors know best

how to get along with Holy Mother Earth.

Animists believe in a fundamental unity of all life in the cosmos. Spirit and matter are often the same; vegetable and mineral life may contain the kind of soul that man does; people can change (or be changed) into animals and trees, and so on. There's no point in mortal woman or man thinking they are any better or more important than any other living (or non-living) thing in the universe, of course, since essences are so transient and changeable.

Modern druids (following in the footsteps of the ancient ones) celebrate the Midsummer festival at Stonehenge, England.

'Man is the only animal that blushes. Or needs to.'
Mark Twain

'Man is Creation's master-piece; but who says so?'
Elbert Hubbard

● **Man and woman are God's special and unique creation.** Made in God's own image, they are endowed with God-like qualities. Loved by God, they are infinitely valuable. Human beings are the crown of creation.

● **Man and woman are evil.** Although created for good, they have constantly chosen evil. Basic human nature is depraved — every human action shows innate wickedness.

Obviously, balancing these two beliefs is difficult. Although both are true in certain respects, according to orthodox Christian thought, the challenge of holding the two ideas in the mind simultaneously is greater than can be met by most. As a result, two broad opinions are often expressed:

As a loved creation of God, created to be like God, humankind is by nature a God-like and a good creation. It's true that people don't always do the 'right' thing, but that's more because of corruption in human systems and societies than any flaw in their own nature. Freed from the restrictions of an oppressive society, allowed to flourish, allowed to exercise their creativity, their beauty and light will shine, showing humans to be tremendously kind and wonderfully inventive.

As much as we might like to believe it, a quick look at the ways humans have behaved throughout the ages clearly shows that they are the only species that actively calculates the demise of its own, that 'freed from the restrictions of an oppressive society,' they would quickly destroy themselves and much of the rest of creation. Although humans may have been created for good, they quickly choose evil, and it is in this sorry state — individually and collectively — that we find modern man.

In the end, either point of view, carried to an extreme, will produce a skewed view of the universe. On one hand, a dogmatic belief in innate human goodness will lead to constant disappointment (if not classic existential despair), when people repeatedly do what is bad. After all, optimists and humanists can blame the corruption of society for the failure of mankind to live responsibly and humanely for only so long. Eventually, the humanist viewpoint leads to a dark nihilism: the belief that nothing makes sense, that life is a big, cruel joke, and that humankind is the butt of that joke.

But those who stress fallen human nature will find themselves unable to explain many things. Why a soldier will throw himself on a live grenade in order to save the lives of his comrades. Why an individual will sacrifice his own comfort to help a stranger in need. Or even why a mother will nurse her child. Attempts to pin all acts of bravery, charity, and affection onto personal interest or genetic reflex is, in the end, artificial. Those who believe only in the evil of the human race take on a heavy burden. They find it increasingly difficult to find *any* virtue in themselves or others that could justify either's existence. Again, life emerges as a cruel hoax perpetuated on an unsuspecting victim.

BEING TRULY HUMAN

Christians believe that each of these two views — humans good or humans bad — is important to regulate each other. Both have to be kept in balance, explaining human nature in this way:

When man and woman were created, they were created good, according to the Bible. Then they disobeyed God; they 'fell' from friendship with God. This was the

WHAT YOU SEE IS WHAT YOU GET

The Humanist Manifesto (number 2) asserts: 'We find insufficient evidence for belief in the existence of a supernatural . . .'

And if evidence is unavailable, then surely the possibility of a realm beyond the natural cannot be entertained for long. Naturalist thought claims that physical matter is the only thing that exists. (This is why so many pilgrims are hesitant to enter the New Age without booking in advance.)

The cosmos? It is nothing more than a uniform system of cause and effect, running pretty much under its own steam. The New Age humanist asserts that human beings or God (if God exists, which, judging from the look of things, he doesn't) have no ability to influence or change this closed universe. Obviously, this is a tremendous departure from those beliefs that live or die on the assumption that the workings of the universe can be manipulated by magic, mind control or other human efforts.

Each human being is also a system of cause and effect, just like the universe. A mini-system. What we call the personality, or the self, is merely a complex interaction of various chemical and physical properties, none of which are fully understood — yet. And when you die . . . zip! That's it. You're dead. There is just no good, objective reason to believe that life in any form continues after this one is over. In other words, there is no 'invisible universe' or 'Mind-at-Large,' for the simple reason that such theories are unobservable and unmeasurable, and therefore unthinkable.

For many pilgrims this is a fairly obtuse way to think. 'I can't see this as being truly New Age,' they say. 'Seems more Scientific Age to me.'

The fact is that for a great many people the New Age can properly begin only when the naturalist point of view is adopted in every field of endeavor. All disciplines must subject themselves to the laws of scientific inquiry, theory and method, which states that if something can be observed and measured in some way, it exists. If it cannot, it does not. Phenomena that appear inexplicable are merely lacking proper scientific investigation.

But given time (and sufficient funding) increased knowledge of the physical laws governing the universe will eventually explain everything in a sensible, rational way, tie up all loose ends, and answer all questions. Amen.

The world's largest array of radio telescopes at Socorro, New Mexico. Alongside their optical counterparts, radio telescopes have mapped out vast areas of knowledge about the Universe.

beginning of our checkered humanity as we now know it. God forever strives to bring us back into fellowship with himself. His last and most strenuous attempt was by becoming a human being himself in the person of Jesus — for the purpose of reconciling man's evil to God's good.

These central Christian beliefs can help us, even in the New Age, to make sense of the evil and the good in human beings. Put into a diagram, men and women are . . .

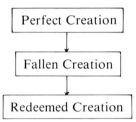

All three parts of this equation work together. If we accept as a fact that the human race is fallen, then we must believe we were originally created good — since you cannot fall unless you have someplace to fall from. And if the human race never fell, how can we be redeemed? There is no need to fix something that isn't broken! On the other hand, why go to the considerable trouble of redeeming something that's worthless? Fallen man must still contain some spark of the divine, or God would simply have scrubbed us out and started again long ago.

Placing perfect/fallen/redeemed man and woman back in the cosmos, then, it's clearer to us now how we got in the muddle we're in.

It's obvious that we have been less than prudent in our management of the universe — in both a physical and moral sense. We have failed to live responsibly in many ways.

Nevertheless, that fact does not negate our right to belong in the cosmos. A child who is given a beautiful new coat by his parents, and who decides to cut a hole in it, does not necessarily forfeit his rights of ownership. Rather, he is in the sad situation of owning a beautiful coat with a nasty hole in it, with no one but himself to blame for this unhappy state of affairs.

As God's unique creation, we are accountable to God for the way we behave on this Earth. The Earth will tell on us if we persist in behaving recklessly. There will be no way to cover our tracks, and no one to blame but ourselves. And God, who put us here to run the show, so to speak, will ultimately demand a personal accounting.

ME, MYSELF, AND I

The cosmos, admittedly an exceedingly huge place, is perhaps no larger in its scope than the New Age self. For in the New Age, the self is paramount. Man-as-unwelcome-guestism notwithstanding, the idea that the self is the only important reality is perhaps *the* major tenet of New Age thinking.

We have for generations believed that an individual's existence was rooted in his or her past. A young man took the occupation of his father, who had taken the occupation of his father before him. A young woman relied on her parents to choose an appropriate husband for her, and devoted her life to raising children, as her own mother had. The idea that 'there is nothing new under the sun' was affirmed time and again in practice and belief.

The present generation believes, however, that its existence is rooted in the *future*. Not content to repeat the mistakes of the past (or even sift wisdom from them), New Agers look to the future to provide answers to the problems of the present. They optimistically believe that we can change our conscious selves, our character, our very essence. Humankind can not only evolve, it can be transformed.

'There is as much difference between us and ourselves as between us and others.'
Michel de Montaigne

Sigmund Freud reading in his study in 1938, the year before his death. Freud has been called 'the father of psychoanalysis'. He is one of the few men who have had a deep and lasting influence on 20th century thinking.

But transformation demands an increased depth of self-understanding. The New Age vocabulary contains words and concepts virtually unheard of at the turn of the 20th century, words such as ideal self, real self, self-image, self-esteem, self-acceptance, self-concept, self-actualization, self-determination and self-fulfilment.

'Just what is the "self"?' ask concerned pilgrims. 'Will I recognize it when I see it?' Most New Agers, vitally concerned with self-discovery, have a ready definition. The self is generally considered to be that delightful bundle of conscious awareness we know ourselves to be.

That undoubtedly sounds vague. Nevertheless, since the self is everything — since it's the existential kingpin — then whatever you believe to be self *is* self, and that decision is final. The word defines itself.

If that doesn't give you a place to hang your hat, you might like to imagine the self looking like the heart of a big, multi-petalled daisy.

Where desires, perceptions, needs and so on converge, the self exists. When a person says 'I' or 'me,' that's self.

With that much by way of definition, then, the tour will journey briefly to the not-too-distant past — with high hopes of understanding the present. How did we arrive at a world filled to the brim with personal selves, a world in which each individual's 'me' has become the pre-eminent concern? What should every conscientious pilgrim understand about the self?

THE HAUNTED HOUSE

We begin with an excursion into the home of the world-famous creator of the psychoanalytic school of psychology, Sigmund Freud.

Freud lived in a fairly dark, somewhat musty, decidedly untidy old

Victorian mansion. The house was built on the belief that man is himself basically a dark, musty and untidy creature, whose mind is a mazework haunted by the shadows of past traumas, by primal impulses that wilfully assert themselves given half a chance, and by wicked thoughts that strain at their chains in a never-ending effort to dominate the personality.

In order to understand the tortured human self and to develop cures for its numerous ills, Freud atomized the personality, breaking it apart into its most basic components, believing, like all good doctors, that a thorough examination of the various parts would detect the malfunctioning member.

● **The Id,** he theorized, is the basic core of the personality. We are born with a fully developed Id; it is all our inherited characteristics, our animal instincts. It is concerned primarily with avoiding pain and obtaining pleasure.

● **The Ego** is that part of the personality that attempts to reconcile the prodigal Id with the more conservative demands of living. The Ego is supremely pragmatic, endowed with the invaluable ability to distinguish what exists merely in the mind from nuts-and-bolts reality. Information of this sort is extremely useful and important to the self, because it helps the Id do its job — avoid pain and obtain pleasure — since confusing illusion with reality is certain to lead to disaster. And disaster is, as we all know, nearly always excruciatingly painful.

● **The Superego** is that part of the personality which strives for perfection — as opposed to avoiding pain and obtaining pleasure (Id) or creating a protective buffer between

the Id and the more painful aspects of reality (Ego). The Superego's job is to keep the Id under control (you never know what Id will do if left alone for a minute!), to encourage the Ego to act in a moral way (the Ego's preoccupation with cold, hard reality might overlook the ethical consequences of certain courses of action), and to strive for overall perfection.

If that sounds confusing, don't worry. It *is*. And that's just the beginning of Freud's many complex theories about the self, which he likened to an iceberg. In the case of an iceberg, of course, only the tip of it can be seen, while 90% of its mass remains hidden beneath the water's surface. And so it is with the human self, argued Freud. If you want to understand why humans do what they do, you must be willing to find ways to investigate the vast, hidden reaches of the human self.

So Freud's house contains many secret passages, many closets, many dark corridors and many surprises for the houseguest who decides to venture out of the confines of his room in

A dusty, cluttered, mysterious Victorian house with hidden corners, unknown doors and dark cellars. Rather like the human mind . . .

search of self-enlightenment. Displaced objects, sublimated expressions, defense mechanisms, haunting projections, reaction formations, repression and regression are all present in the home of Sigmund Freud, as they are in the personality of man.

Many brilliant psychologists lived with Freud in his house; they were devoted to his teachings, and to the mysteries he was able to unlock, the doors he was able to open with his theories and methods of inquiry. But eventually, most of them left the house, either evicted for the sin of questioning some of Freud's more outlandish theories (he often diagnosed such heretics as insane), or merely preferring to build their own, more modern houses. True, they took with them many of Freud's furnishings, and even in their rebellion confessed their debt to Freud's taste in decor.

'I can't figure out where I leave off and everyone else begins.'
George McCabee

Most of them envisioned a house less dark and shadowy, a house built upon the loftier premise that men, if not basically good, was at least morally neutral. They sought to move the understanding of the self into a different neighborhood, one where the theorist was not forced to spend tedious hours preoccupied with the bad parts of human beings, but where they could spend time exploring the basic goodness of humanity. Enter: *The New Age Self*.

THE ENLIGHTENED A-FRAME

Of the many psychologists and psychiatrists who left Freud's home to build their own abodes, one of the most influential was Abraham Maslow. His structure could best be characterized as an A-frame house, with spacious rooms, comfortable furnishings, large picture windows, and a sunny view to the south.

He wholeheartedly rejected the idea that humanity was basically bad, and that the personality was hidden in shadows. 'You've been looking too long at the few people who are psychotic and disordered,' he told Freud and the others who lived in Freud's house. 'I will look at normal people. Even more, I will look at people who have achieved great

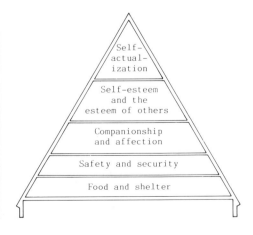

Self-actual-ization

Self-esteem and the esteem of others

Companionship and affection

Safety and security

Food and shelter

success. I will converse with happy, fulfilled, creative, interesting people, and by studying them, I will be able to build a house that can contain the theories necessary to explain *their* behavior.'

So he set about his task, convinced that the self is not an Id/Ego/Superego dynamism, but a whole, a unified entity, with an integrity of its own. This whole self strives for one thing — self-actualization.

Self-actualization: the fulfilment of one's deepest potentials.

Fulfilment: satisfaction, completion.

Potentials: possibilities; latent, unrealized or undeveloped capabilities.

Of course, self-actualization is not often achieved. When it is not, it is because the environment or circumstances have conspired to prevent its realization. It is required of individuals and society at large to create an environment where the self can flourish, where it can become actualized.

Any individual who climbs to the top floor — the pinnacle of self-actualization — requires first the satisfaction of basic needs: food, clothing, shelter and protection. Then there is further progress.

Many people, alas, never make it to the highest level of Maslow's house. They fall on the steep flights of stairs, victims of the loose treads of circumstance. But a few advance themselves to the point where they become self-actualized. Maslow found on the upper level of his house achievers like Abraham Lincoln, Albert Einstein, Thomas Jefferson, Henry David Thoreau, Eleanor Roosevelt and Ludwig von Beethoven.

Still, something was missing for the self-actualized individual. Having obtained nearly everything worth obtaining, the actualized self still felt a need for transcendence, still felt a need to be at one with the cosmos. The solution to this problem? To punch a hole in the roof, to break out of the house via the skylight and see the face of God in unitive consciousness, to commune directly with the essence of all being.

Abraham Lincoln, Eleanor Roosevelt, Thoreau and Beethoven: four self-actualized heroes from Abraham Maslow's gallery.

THE HUMAN POTENTIAL MOVEMENT

One experiment in skylight-breaking was begun at the Esalen Institute in the Big Sur area of Northern California.

(Pilgrims often wonder why it is that so many of the New Age journeys originate in California. Perhaps the balmy weather and unfettered lifestyle on the western coast of the United States influences the inhabitants to think innovatively, non-stereotypically and idiosyncratically. Maybe it's more than coincidence that the part of the United States furthest from Europe (and European logic) and closest to Asia (and Oriental mysticism) is midwife to some of the more fascinating hybrids of East-meets-West philosophy. It could be that sun, surf and sailboards have an intrinsic power to influence all who come within their range. However it is, a great deal of New Age thinking has been formulated in California.)

Meanwhile, back in Esalen . . . Aldous Huxley founded a retreat center with his friends that kindled what is now referred to as the human potential movement. In the early years of its existence (1961 on) it attracted such luminaries as Carl Rogers, Arnold Toynbee, Linus Pauling, Paul Tillich, Rollo May and Carlos Castaneda as participants and visiting lecturers. True believers see no coincidence in the fact that a heavy fog in the area once brought a vacationing Abraham Maslow to seek shelter at Esalen for the night with the result that he, too, became (by design? by accident?) a part of the movement.

What is the human potential movement? Its scope was and is broadly defined, but generally it is

devoted to discovering ways in which the full power, the full potential of the human self, can be released for the fulfilment of the individual and the benefit of society. Encounter groups, seminars, lectures and informal bull sessions engaging some of the most fertile minds in the world explored all avenues of possibility.

The mood was definitely up-beat. And why not? In the United States of the early 1960s, President Lyndon B. Johnson was pushing through Congress the most revolutionary civil rights legislation since the Emancipation Proclamation, and declaring 'war on poverty.' The Free Speech Movement at nearby Berkeley, the beginnings of sexual liberation, heightened concern for the disenfranchised minorities, and Martin Luther King's leadership in the civil rights movement were part of the spirit of the times.

With such dramatic political and social happenings pulling down the walls that separated people, the human potential movement would meet that action with its own, breaking down the barriers between mind and body, integrating the wisdom of the East with the pragmatism of the West, transforming the atomized self into a holistic self, ready to meet the New Age.

Esalen spawned similar

HAPPINESS, INC.

Norman Vincent Peale championed the cause of self-esteem for many with his book *The Power of Positive Thinking*. An immediate success in 1952, and a worldwide bestseller to this day, its thesis is that high self-esteem, subsequent self-confidence, a cheery outlook and a discipline of positive thinking will make a success of any person. The chapter titles in this book give a taste of its contents: 'Believe in Yourself' 'How to Create Your Own Happiness . . .' 'Expect the Best and Get It . . .' 'I Don't Believe in Defeat . . .' 'How to Get People to Like You . . .' 'How to Draw upon That Higher Power . . .'

The charisma the Rev Dr Peale exuded in the book made converts of millions. Everyday sorts of people (not the kind likely to devote two weeks to a Gestalt encounter therapy group at Esalen to receive similar encouragement) came under his influence, applying these principles to their lives. And — apparently — they discovered that a positive mental outlook did indeed make success obtainable (or defeat less painful).

The baton has recently been passed from Dr Peale to Dr Robert Schuller, senior minister of California's Garden Grove Community Church, the first drive-in church in America, home of the fabulous multi-million dollar Crystal Cathedral and the weekly television broadcast of the Sunday morning service which is called *Hour of Power*.

'Possibility thinkers is what we need today,' proclaims Dr Schuller. His

Robert Schuller's Crystal Cathedral.

book *Move Ahead With Possibility Thinking* is peppered with idiomatic advice:
- Problems are guidelines, not stop signs!
- Great ideas attract big people.
- The difficult we do immediately — the impossible takes a little longer.
- Self-confidence is security!

By the time that Dr Schuller has postulated that 'When you catch up with your goals you are in trouble!' those who are less than gung-ho are wondering if there's any way *out* of possibility thinking!

In his more recent book, *Self-Esteem: The New Reformation*, Dr Schuller seems also to have a mental picture of Maslow's enlightened A-Frame in his mind, postulating that self-esteem (or lack of it) is what is standing between the average modern person and a full understanding of God. So Schuller, too, tries to blow the roof off the top of Maslow's house, seeing lack of self-esteem as a barrier that separates us from God.

communities devoted to finding the latent energy in the human self, and once and for all established California as the hub of the human potential movement, as the pace-setter for the world in new philosophies, novel lifestyles, and original thinking.

The imperative for self-actualization — the fulfilment of human potential — has quickly spread to areas far outside the psychological realm. The self, after all, is one's very essence, and the achievement of anything an individual sets out to do is determined by the self.

It is clear to see that there are few self-actualized people in the world. Only a small percentage have even begun to realize their complete human potential. What can be done so that there are more fulfilled folks?

Looking back to the diagram of Maslow's house, it's not hard to see that the well-heeled New Age pilgrim has food and shelter, safety and security, companionship and affection. But what's this? He is lacking *self-esteem!* But of course! Having achieved all basic needs, he lacks only that which will make him feel good about his achievements.

The New Age rationalist declares: 'The idea that mankind is evil has been so pervasive in past generations that we are stuck with a world full of people who simply don't view themselves in a favorable light. People don't *like* themselves.' The theory is thus established: **a person who doesn't like him or herself is incapable of liking others.**

The rider to this theory is: It is necessary that a person develop a high degree of self-esteem in order to have esteem for others and to become a fully actualized individual.

Necessary? It is the individual's *duty*. We owe it to ourselves and to our fellow human beings to fulfil our needs and desires, to hold a lofty opinion of ourselves, to cherish ourselves — for the good of all.

THE 'ME' GENERATION

Some attribute it to the failure of the political activism of young people in the 1960s to effect any kind of significant social change. Others say that it's the natural response to an increasingly depersonalized, technological society. A few believe that a depressed world economy is to blame, that the shortage of petroleum, the depletion of natural resources, and a shifting balance of trade is responsible.

Responsible for what?

Responsible for the fact that people all over the world have, of late, been more and more preoccupied with themselves and less concerned with others. Tom Wolfe called the 1970s (in America, at least) the 'Me Decade,' succinctly summing up the narcissistic self-regard with which we held ourselves.

The Me Generation has its creed, canonized by gestalt therapist Fritz Perls:

I do my own thing, and you do your thing.
I am not in this world to live up to your expectations.
And you are not in this world to live up to mine.
You are you and I am I.
And if by chance we find each other, it's beautiful.
If not, it can't be helped.

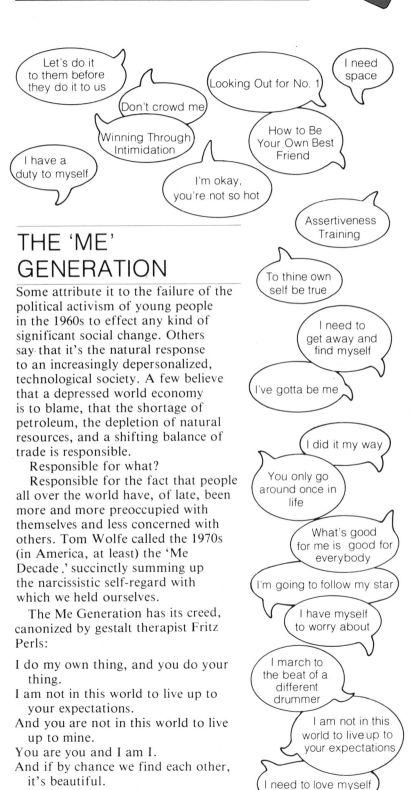

Images of the Sixties.
Left: psychedelic fashions. Above:
Beatlemania hits Los Angeles. Below:
flower-power on the street of New
York.

Of course, narcissistic self-absorption is the natural outcome of a psycho-philosophy based on the notion that the self is created by the self; that self-esteem leads to self-actualization leads to cosmic consciousness; that the self-determined individual can make a difference in the world; that in order to have concern for others one must first have concern for oneself.

What was begun with Norman Vincent Peale, Robert Schuller, Abraham Maslow and Esalen (not in that order, but all at the same time) and hosts of others, found its way into the collective consciousness of the New Age, an intoxicating wine that had been aging for years.

The result? The result was Werner Erhard's *est* (Erhard Seminars Training), where roomfuls of people subjected themselves to humiliation, verbal abuse, physical discomfort, and the subtlest of behavior control techniques in hopes of getting 'it.'

Said Erhard of his course in 'personal growth': 'It elevates you from being the effect of your circumstances to being the cause of your circumstances . . . When you get in touch with yourself — not with your position and not with your ego and not with your point of view, but with yourself . . . you will experience yourself as the creator of your own circumstance.'

DOWN FROM THE MOUNTAIN

Transcendental Meditation (TM) is yet another New Age practice trading on the idea that human beings are one with creation, one with the gods and one with universal cosmic consciousness. It is, to date, the most successful attempt to translate Eastern thought for Western minds.

TM is the religion/philosophy/discipline that originated with the Maharishi Mahesh Yogi. The Maharishi based it on years of study with his beloved teacher, Guru Dev, personification of the Hindu deities Vishnu, Brahma and Shiva.

In 1957, after Guru Dev died, the Maharishi decided to launch Transcendental Meditation in India. But India already had as many yogi-type philosophies and religions as it could absorb and more to spare, so Mahesh decided to seek greener pastures elsewhere, beginning with the United States. He came to Los Angeles in 1959, and stayed for a couple of years, returning to India in 1961 to devise the method by which he would introduce his meditation philosophy to the entire world.

An excellent stroke of luck came his way in 1967 when he met — the Beatles. Blast Off! Transcendental Meditation and the Maharishi got just the boost they needed. Basking in the same limelight that followed the Fab Four wherever they went, he was skyrocketed to success. Celebrated in popular song, the guest of honor on talk-shows, and a cult figure with the young, he and his teaching caught on like measles.

One of the basic tenets of the 'Science of Creative Intelligence' (TM) is that the world will not change us; rather, it is we who must change ourselves. As changed people we can then change the world. The Maharishi called this current epoch of history the Age of Enlightenment, reiterating what other New Age thinkers have maintained all along: that one way or another, it is possible and necessary for human beings to be transformed, so that the world can be transformed, not destroyed.

The main tool for transformation is meditation (ideally, two twenty-minute periods per day), in which the devotee meditates on his or her *mantra* (a supposedly meaningless Sanskrit word, known only to the meditator and the teacher who gives it to him or her). By concentrating on the *mantra*, the meditator will eventually and inevitably achieve selfhood. This is done by diving through the *awareness* level of thought, into the *subconscious* levels of thought, and right down to the *source of thought* which is *pure awareness* — that is, being, the self, which, paradoxically, can only be realized through individual extinction.

And as if that wasn't enough, TMers are promised decreased stress, increased productivity, heightened creativity, and overall peace of mind.

While strenuously denying any ties with religion, and at the same time asserting compatibility with any and all religious beliefs the meditator may happen to bring with him, TM nevertheless bears all the earmarks of religion. It has a messiah figure (The Maharishi, called 'his holiness'); institutionalization (a very complex system of societies, foundations, training schools and administrative bureaucracies); homogenization of adherents; a stringent doctrine; a commitment to evangelize and obtain converts; and religious mystique and symbolism (flowing robes, secret mystic words, decorated altars and sacrifices of flowers and fruit to pictures of Guru Dev and the Maharishi).

The popularity of TM has waned in recent years. Perhaps the claim that made it so popular in the first place — that meditators need not give up any previously-held religious beliefs or make any drastic lifestyle changes — has backfired. An easy-to-accept philosophy is also easy-to-neglect. TM has attracted hordes of people who don't want to give up much in their search for peace of mind and awareness of self. They often find that when nothing is sacrificed, nothing is gained, either. So, they leave as quickly as they came.

The Maharishi Mahesh Yogi with his two most celebrated disciples, Beatles George Harrison and John Lennon.

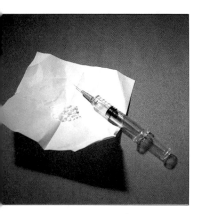

Dr Timothy Leary and others in the 1960s advocated the use of drugs to expand the mind. Drugs like heroin have made millionaires out of the evil men who operate international drug trails, and have destroyed those who use them.

'The living self has one purpose only: to come into its own fullness of being, as a tree comes into full blossom, or a bird into spring beauty, or a tiger into lustre.'
D.H.Lawrence

The result? A militant narcissism, apparent in books for up-and-coming fast-track business executives with titles like *Dress for Success, Winning Through Intimidation*, and *Looking Out For No. 1*. Women, especially, availed themselves of courses in assertiveness training, where they were taught how to express and insist upon their own point of view, standing up to the power structure (namely, a male-dominated society) demanding respect.

The result? A cult of self-discovery that revolved around the use of hallucinogenic and other mind-expanding chemicals in order to unlock the true inner essence of the self. Turn on and tune in, find out who you are with LSD, mescaline, hashish, marijuana, and other consciousness-altering drugs.

The result? A renewed interest in psychotherapy, to the extent that it could uncover the true self and explain its workings. No longer limited to being solely a tool to help the troubled gain mental health (which it never really did very well anyway), analysis became the pastime of relatively healthy (and wealthy) people. Journaling, dream interpretation, guided imagery, hypnosis and primal therapy were employed to unlock the past, present and future, presenting it to the individual seeking a more complete definition of his or her true self.

The result? Transcendental Meditation.

HAVE YOU FULFILLED YOUR SELF-POTENTIAL TODAY?

The self movement will continue to flourish for many years. Its location, definition and character may change slightly in the coming years, as it has

in the past, but the hope of achieving self-actualization is far too alluring to be easily abandoned.

Perhaps the most persistent claim of the self movement is that each person is, to a very great extent, the master of her or his own destiny, the creator of a unique self, the possessor of an all-powerful will that determines the quality of existence. Each individual is *duty-bound* to seek actualization.

The responsibility for self-determination, and the duty-to-self ethic is, regrettably, every bit as burdensome as the old self-denial ethic it was meant to replace. How can anyone live up to all of one's vast, bewildering, often conflicting and contradictory needs, desires, potentials, opportunities and expectations? It would be a full-time occupation for any dozen individuals.

The human potential movement places an unbearable load on the poor, lone soul who is morally obligated to fulfil, fulfil, fulfil — regardless of whether such fulfilment is constructive for him or his society.

It is also evident that the search for the self is, using Maslow's model, a pastime for a privileged few. There isn't a great deal of time or energy for deep and elaborate introspection for the person who is forced to spend most of his or her waking moments obtaining food for the day, or shelter for the night — according to Maslow.

Ironically, though, the belief exists that each of us (as the possessor of a unique and special self), regardless of our economic position, can find fulfilment in whatever circumstances we find ourselves. Surely we believe the current folk wisdom that tells us the poor and simple of this world are often more 'together' than the confused and idle rich?

GOD AND MAN, SELF-TO-SELF

The Christian faith holds the human self in very high esteem, asserting that each human creation is precious in the sight of God, loved personally by God, and inexpressibly valuable.

While touring the Cosmos we pointed out that humankind was created good by God, that humankind rebelled against God, and that in time God used his Son, Jesus Christ, to reconcile this rebellious creation to his perfect self. We also pointed out that this reconciliation was initiated because human beings were originally created in the image of God. People possessed an element of the divine in their nature, and were eminently worth restoring.

Christianity (and Judaism, from which it sprang) is distinctive in worshipping a God who is a 'self'. The Christian God is not a force of nature, not a state of mind, not a spiritual fog or energy ball loose in the universe, not a state of perfection or unity to be obtained by any amount of personal discipline or striving. God is not an 'it'. God is a person. God has a personality. God has emotions. God has desires, perceptions and will, and even needs. God, according to the Bible, has everything necessary to constitute a 'self'.

The human self is patterned after the design of God's self and is therefore somewhat divine. True, the self is made up of our choices throughout our lifetime, of our environmental conditions, of our life experiences. But, at the same time, this self is not completely of our own making, as Maslow would claim. We are incapable of creating a self on our own. In a very real sense, our own, unique, individualized selves are given to us by God's greater, infinite self. They are bestowed upon us by a loving Creator.

Where does this leave the ongoing search for self-fulfilment? To the extent that self-fulfilment becomes a quest to fill every desire of the heart (many of which are bound to be competing and contradictory), self-fulfilment is a futile search. There is simply no way a human being can actualize every potential, meet every desire, or fill every need he or she possesses. Certain needs and desires must be suppressed or abandoned so that others may be fulfilled.

Jesus once said, 'Whoever finds his life will lose it, and whoever loses his life for my sake will find it.' From a purely practical point of view, the idea of *losing* yourself so that you can *find* yourself makes a great deal of sense. It is in harmony with the facts of life.

Beyond that, the Christian faith recognizes that each person is, indeed, a spiritual being, and that only by seeking communion with the self of God (the source of humanness), is it

The western world stresses the importance of the individual. But it is also true that we can discover who we really are in community. To be human means to belong to the human race.

possible to be fully a human self.

As for Maslow's hierarchy of needs, the usefulness of his model is limited. The bright and sunny A-frame begins to take on the aspect of a modern-day Tower of Babel, which is what the ancients built to reach to the heavens and, ultimately, immortality. The project led only to confusion, not to heaven, as God hampered their efforts by confusing their language so the bewildered builders couldn't communicate with one another on their ill-conceived project.

Self-actualization does not lead to knowledge of God. Instead, the reverse is true: knowledge of and submission to God leads to the complete realization of self, and possibly its actualization. Christians believe that, regardless of whether or not a person's even most basic needs are met, that person is a fully actualized person if he or she has made the decision to abandon him or herself to faith in God.

Self-esteem comes from God. It is the realization of personal worth we receive once we understand that God, Creator of the Universe and Ultimate Self, made each of us, individually, in the image of himself and loved us enough to sacrifice the life of his only Son so that our rebellion would no longer separate us from him.

This assurance is a cosmic constant. It is not altered by others' opinions of us, our own self-image, our successes or failures in life, or anything else. It is absolute. And it is a fact, whether anyone believes it or not.

The Apostle Paul expressed this when he said, 'I am convinced that neither death nor life, neither angels nor demons, neither the present nor the future, nor any powers, neither height nor depth, nor anything else in all creation, will be able to separate us from the love of God that is in Christ Jesus our Lord.'

Since each individual is intimately involved with God on a self-to-self basis, the next fact follows automatically: each human self is connected to each other human self.

This is what Maslow himself eventually realized. By the time a self-actualized person reached the top floor of his hierarchical A-frame, he was pretty much alone, and he knew it. Even the superior, self-actualized person has a need to relate intimately with other people.

Yes, the self does express itself. But this expression can be seen mainly in relationship with other people. The idea that you can find yourself simply by becoming isolated physically (hermit-style) for an extended period of time is not true. The fact of the matter is that, aside from brief periods of solitude for meditation, reflection, and rejuvenation, the self can exist in completeness only when it breaks out of its isolation and relates intimately with others.

Which brings us to the next leg of our journey: the family.

TORONTO
Charles and Ellen's marriage is the second for both of them. Their children by previous marriages, five in all, live with them. The household population varies from day to day, as the children leave to spend time with the non-custodial parents. When grandparents, step-grandparents, uncles and aunts, step-uncles and -aunts, and other members of their extended family are present, the count can swell to twenty or more people. They see their family life as sometimes confusing, but fulfilling.

STOCKHOLM
Kjell and Anna have been married for five years and desperately want a child. Anna cannot conceive, so through their lawyer the couple has contacted a young woman who will bear a child for them. The surrogate mother will be artificially inseminated with Kjell's sperm and the resulting child will be adopted by the couple, who have agreed to pay the mother a generous sum. They consider it a small price to pay for having a family at last.

JOHANNESBURG
William has severe physical handicaps that require professional attendance. At twenty-two, he left the home of his father and mother to live in a group home with other physically handicapped people. His family consists of two specially trained houseparents and three other young people about his age. His parents travel from a nearby town to visit him about once a month.

GOLAN
Uriel is a seventeen-year-old boy who lives in a kibbutz. He was born in the kibbutz, and after he finishes school and military service, will return to the kibbutz. Uriel has lived in a dormitory with other children his age since he was eighteen-months old. He sees his parents every day after school, and during their free time from work. Living in the kibbutz is like being part of a huge family, says Uriel, with many brothers and sisters, aunts and uncles.

LOS ANGELES

Tory, an eight-year-old boy, comes directly home from school at 3:15, lets himself into the apartment, fixes himself an afternoon snack, and calls his father at the office. After checking in, he does an hour of homework, and then watches television until his father gets home from work, usually about 5:30 or 6:00. Tory often gets dinner started by placing a casserole in the oven or making a salad for the two of them. He knows he is an important part of his family.

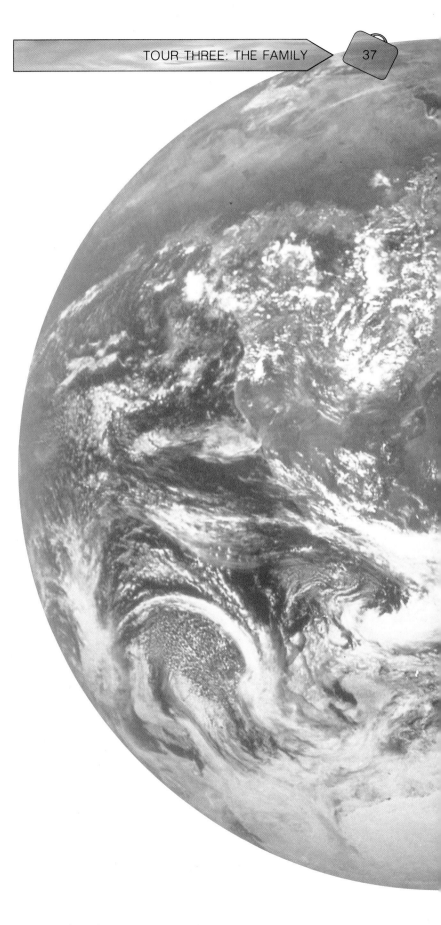

PARIS

Emma is a 73-year-old widow who lives alone. Her three children all live in the metropolitan area: two are married with children, one is divorced with no children. She has, at times, considered the possibility of living with one of her children because her pension is barely adequate to cover her basic living expenses. She has never brought up the subject with any of her children, since she has vowed never to become a burden to her family.

LIVERPOOL

Living on government benefit, Elizabeth is barely able to support herself and her five-month-old daughter, Bridget. Bridget's father has never been married to Elizabeth and provides no financial support for his child, although he does drop by to see her occasionally. Elizabeth plans to stay home until Bridget is in school, believing that it is important for a mother to spend time with her children.

DALLAS

Janet and Bill have been married for thirteen years; she is a counseling psychologist with a successful private practice, and he is a real estate lawyer. They have three children, ages eleven, seven, and two. The eleven-year-old attends a private boarding school, coming home weekends and during holidays to be with the family. A live-in maid cares for the younger children and keeps house while Janet and Bill pursue their busy schedules — which often see them away from home twelve to fourteen hours a day. They speak of themselves as a typical American family.

NEW YORK

When Carole's company offered her a promotion that would require relocating in the Chicago area, she and her husband Jeff decided to become a commuting couple. Thus, they maintain their home in New York City, where Jeff has a good dental practice, and Carole keeps a small apartment in Chicago. She flies home to New York for three days on alternating weekends. Married twenty-three years, they long ago decided that their dual-career marriage precluded having children.

OSLO

Britt is a 43-year-old woman who enjoys her life as a single person. Recognizing that her child-bearing years were almost at an end, she made the decision to conceive a child by artificial insemination. Her daughter Andrea is now 3½ years old, and Britt is generally pleased with her decision to start a family.

'Where does the family start? It starts with a young man falling in love with a girl - no superior alternative has yet been found.'
Winston Churchill

FAMILY FISSION AND FUSION

In Tour One (*The Cosmos*) we saw how the atom, believed for millennia to be the indivisible, most basic building block of all matter, is now known to be a bundle of particles that contains many even-smaller components, some still in the process of being defined. New properties of the atom are manifesting themselves, and strange hybrids and mutants have appeared.

Similarly, the family — traditionally viewed as the indivisible, most basic building block of civilization — is being redefined. All over the world, in nearly every modern society, the family is taking on a different character to the one which it once had. New properties of marriage and family relationships are being discovered, and new possibilities are coming to light. In the New Age, the family is being reformed and transformed. It is evolving and, in some cases, it is mutating.

Like the atom, the fission and fusion of the traditional family unit is creating explosions in our personal lives, doing violence to our society, and generating fall-out that will plague us for generations.

THE REBORN FAMILY

New Age movers and shakers are demanding that technology be brought under control, and that all scientific accomplishments be introduced with respect to — not in spite of — the needs of the human beings living on this planet. They say:

'We're sick and tired of being pulled along by every new technological advance that comes our way. We're tired of playing catch-up with each new discovery, be it the very latest in transportation, communication, education, medication, information or annihilation. From now on, these advances are going to work *for* us, not against us. High quality human life will be the number one priority in the New Age, and technology will be tolerated only to the extent that it creates a humane world in which to live.'

They have a point, of course. Our scientific and technological

According to the Peter Pan Principle*: 'Marriages either peter out or pan out.' For many people, the pressures that used to fall on the supportive family of parents, cousins, aunts and uncles, now fall on unsupported couples.*

achievements are generations ahead of our social institutions. Our knowledge is running far in advance of our ability to assimilate that knowledge into our lives.

For example: It is possible, given the speed of a turbo-jet airliner, for an American couple like Jeff and Carole to have jobs in cities 800 miles apart, to see each other on alternate weekends, and still maintain a home together. But can they survive the isolation and loneliness when they are apart? Is it possible to maintain intimacy long-distance?

It is possible for an unmarried woman like Britt to be artificially inseminated with the sperm of an unknown donor; to conceive and give birth to a healthy infant, all without the help of a husband. But can Britt provide a complete family life as a single parent? Will her child eventually need a father who can be there? Isn't it easier to raise a child with the help and support of a mate?

Reliable birth-control, safe and accessible abortions, large salaries that come with professional jobs, high speed transportation, boarding schools, housekeepers, infertility drugs, surrogate mothers, day-care centers, government subsidies — all these and more are available to the New Age family.

Not only that, the negative social stigma attached to unmarried couples living together, communal living, homosexuality, children conceived outside of marriage, single parenting, and the institutionalization of aged parents is quickly disappearing — if it has not vanished already.

Some view these new trends with satisfaction. 'It's about time,' they say. 'At last we're free of all these old, self-righteous, outdated taboos about what constitutes a legitimate marriage, or a legitimate family. Times are changing. Broader definitions and greater adaptability are what we need now. Of course, this is a transition time for the family, and some people are bound to get hurt when current realities don't meet prior expectations. But in the main, it's for the best. The whole concept of family is being reborn, and I say, let it happen.'

AN INSTITUTION OF SELF-FULFILMENT

Even the most enthusiastic supporters of a New Age family, whatever it will turn out to be, admit that there are serious problems inherent in the reborn family concept: increased divorce; neglected children; unhappy parents; abandoned old people.

The laissez-faire, do-your-own-thing family concept is suffocating the family with high expectations. On the one hand, there are decreased demands on the family to provide financial security, social approval, adult status, or a structure in which to raise children. But on the other hand, the family is currently under a mandate to fuel what, in the New Age, has become the most important, most crucial of all drives — self-fulfilment.

The marriage relationship and the family structure now receive legitimacy from their ability to deliver self-fulfilment. If husband, wife, and children are fulfilled, the relationship is succeeding. If, however, one or more family members are dissatisfied and are not living up to their fullest human potential (or at least approaching it) the family is failing. Believing that love of oneself is the first step to loving another, it follows that a marriage or family situation cannot be considered healthy unless it allows each participant to love and indulge him or herself to the full.

Here's just one illustration of how times have changed. The inability of a wife to bear children has been automatic grounds for divorce in many traditional cultures. After all, what's a woman good for if not to

Catherine of Aragon: divorced, but didn't lose her head over it.

present the husband with heirs — *male* heirs. If she was unable or (worse yet) unwilling to perform that function the marriage was null and void.

Henry VIII divorced Catherine of Aragon for the sin of failing to produce a male heir. Granted, not everyone — most notably, the Pope — agreed with his line of reasoning, but there you have it. Actually, Henry's response was much like the response of today's moderns: if it's hard to win the game, try changing the rules. He did exactly that, of course, breaking away from the established church to establish his own — with himself as the head, and with new rules about divorce that allowed him to play the game *his* way.

Today, infertility is not generally accepted as a valid reason for divorce. The modern wife (or husband) is more likely to be charged with being 'unsupportive' or 'sexually incompatible'. Maybe she isn't 'growing' at her husband's pace, or she's growing in a direction opposite to him. The deficiency of such a wife is that she is not helping her husband to find self-fulfilment. In any number of ways, she is keeping him from being everything he can and consequently should be. Now, *that's* grounds for divorce.

Children, too, may be viewed as obstacles to self-fulfilment. The large investment of time, effort and money that children require has caused many couples to decide that they will remain childless, since they cannot pursue their own professional careers and personal development plans with the added burden of children. The freedom of being a married non-parent is cherished by many. Children, whose presence inhibits their parents' ability to devote themselves whole-heartedly to their careers, who take valuable time away from personal pursuits, who sap the energy of adults, who require money that could be (better) used to furnish a home or travel abroad, are seen as one of the biggest obstacles to self-fulfilment.

If children are desired, or if they are already on the scene when the adults in the family wake up to the possibilities of self-fulfilment, they can (in the New Age) be more conveniently relegated to the care of another. The ever-increasing number of day-care centers and nursery schools are a testament to the fact that parents often wish for others to assume the tasks of childrearing while they remain free to pursue other goals.

And for those who want children but aren't prepared to entertain the demands of a full-time marriage relationship, the cultural ban against a single person purposefully obtaining a child (through natural conception, artificial insemination, or adoption) is being lifted. In the New Age family, it is the woman's right to have or not to have children, as she chooses — and defy anyone else to presume to have an interest or say in her decision. 'It's my body; it's my life,' she reasons. 'It's my choice to make.' Men, on the other hand, do not have all the physical options that women do, but are nevertheless insisting on their right to have children — with or without a wife to bear one. Single men are

adopting families of their own, or turning to surrogate mothers for help in getting started.

THE REVOLUTIONARY CONCEPT

What we now consider the traditional family is anything but traditional when viewed against the backdrop of history. About 3,000 BC the family started to evolve into a new kind of institution. The change began slowly. It started in the Jewish culture and, by the time Jesus Christ had arrived on the scene — nearly 2,000 years ago — he brought marriage and the family to a place it had never been before. Those who studied under him and followed his work continued to encourage the metamorphosis, and the intervening generations between that time and our own have witnessed the fruits of this slow-motion revolution.

The revolution ultimately brought the human family to a place of prominence, a point of exaltation, creating out of what was once merely a biological convenience and sociological necessity a sacred, holy and precious state ripe with tremendous spiritual implications.

When the smoke cleared, here is what had happened:

1. Women were no longer considered chattel, but became co-equal human beings with their husbands.
2. Children became gifts, a trust given to a married couple by a loving God. They were not to be considered property, a source of cheap workers to exploit, or slaves to do the bidding of parents.
3. The sexual relationship between a man and woman ceased to be merely a biological necessity (like sneezing when the nose itches). Instead it became an expression of intimacy that

mystically joined two people as one, a holy act celebrating life.
4. Faithfulness to one's partner, and to one partner only, were commanded as essential disciplines, with the promise that self-control would lead to increased joy.
5. Men were instructed to love their wives as much as they loved their own bodies. In fact, love — not convenience or convention or interfamilial politics — was considered a valid reason to initiate a marriage.
6. Each member of the family was deemed worthy of respect, nurture, and love.

'A revolution?' you ask. 'What's so revolutionary about that?'

Believe us, pilgrim, it wasn't always thus. The marriage of convenience (perhaps as an alliance between tribes, a device by which to gain power or money), the polygamous and polygenous marriage, and the loveless marriage — all these have been the rule throughout history. Up to now, the Judeo-Christian concepts have provided us with our highest ideal of marriage and the family.

Single-parent families face difficult decisions. Should the parent work to provide good income and security for the child, or stay at home to provide love and emotional support?

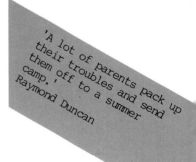

'A lot of parents pack up their troubles and send them off to a summer camp.'
Raymond Duncan

'Insanity is hereditary; you can get it from your children.'
Sam Levenson

Defining the Family

The rights of marriage:

1. To establish the legal father of a woman's children.

2. To establish the legal mother of a man's children.

3. To give the husband a monopoly in the wife's sexuality.

4. To give the wife a monopoly in the husband's sexuality.

5. To give the husband partial or monopolistic rights to the wife's domestic and other labour services.

6. To give the wife partial or monopolistic rights to the husband's labour services.

7. To give the husband partial or total rights over property belonging or potentially accruing to the wife.

8. To give the wife partial or total rights over property belonging or potentially accruing to the husband.

9. To establish a joint fund of property — a partnership — for the benefit of the children of the marriage.

10. To establish a socially significant 'relationship of affinity' between the husband and his wife's brothers.

E. R. Leech, Anthropologist

COVENANTS AND CONTRACTS

Under the Christian system, marriage is not considered a contract, but rather a covenant.

A contract is an agreement between two parties, either spoken or unspoken, to perform certain acts in return for certain considerations. In a contractual marriage, John and Marsha each agree to do and provide certain things. For example, it may be understood by John that Marsha will be available for him sexually; Marsha understands that John will provide financial security for the family; and the children will be seen and not heard.

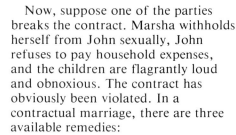

Now, suppose one of the parties breaks the contract. Marsha withholds herself from John sexually, John refuses to pay household expenses, and the children are flagrantly loud and obnoxious. The contract has obviously been violated. In a contractual marriage, there are three available remedies:

● The contract can be revised to accommodate the new situation.

● The situation can be brought in line with the contract.

● The marriage/family can be dissolved by reason of default by the parties involved in the contract.

Now let's consider a covenant relationship. In a covenant, promises are also made, just as they are in a contract. The difference is that the promises are *unconditional*. They are not invalidated if parties to the covenant fail to fulfil expectations.

In a covenant marriage, what happens if Marsha, John and the children all fail to keep certain of their promises to each other? Answer: The marriage proceeds; its survival does not depend on John and Marsha's follow-through on the promises they made. It survives because each member of the covenant relationship is absolutely and unconditionally committed to keeping the covenant.

The wedding ceremony traditionally used in Christian nuptials sums up the covenant relationship of Christian marriage. A close look at them shows that the vows are actually very realistic, not sentimental at all. The relationship is unconditional — for richer *or* poorer, in sickness *and* in health, and so on. It covers nearly all contingencies.

But it is *not* contractual, because it presents no 'out' if things don't go well. There are no loopholes to slip through. There are also no 'I'll do this *if* you do this . . .' clauses. The commitment abides, even when the husband and wife (or unruly children)

'No matter how many communes anybody invents, the family always creeps back.' (Margaret Mead) The family unit has been remarkably resilient down the centuries.

fail to live up to their respective ends of the bargain.

The nature of a covenant relationship is a bit easier to grasp in the case of parents and children. Parents tend to love their children unconditionally. A few parents may give up on their children, but not many, and not easily. Most parents will stick by their kids no matter what. And, conversely, a few children may give up on their parents, leaving home physically or emotionally before reaching maturity. But not many. Most children stick it out with their parents, through thick and thin.

A couple who decide to have a child usually has it in their minds before the birth that they will love and accept the child — *no matter what*! Even if it's a boy (they were so hoping for a girl); even if it's a brunette (they thought she would be blonde); even if he doesn't sleep through the night until he's four; even if he gets rashes, measles and colic — they will be faithful to their child.

So it is with a covenant marriage. Husband and wife will stay with the marriage come what may. It's a promise.

THE METAPHOR

Marriage and the family are common metaphors. We speak of Big Brother, Uncle Sam and Mother Earth, or of a person being married to his job, or giving birth to a new idea.

The family is also a metaphor for God-to-man relationships.

God is spoken of as possessing three distinct aspects: Father, Son, and Holy Spirit. God the Father is portrayed in the Bible as a heavenly parent who gives good things to his children, who disciplines his children, who loves and forgives his children. God also takes on a maternal aspect when compared to a mother caring for her children, or a hen her chicks.

Jesus is called the Son of God (and also the Son of Man). Those who love God are called his children, joint-heirs with Jesus Christ. Christ called himself a bridegroom, and his Church (those who believe what Christ said and take it to heart) is his bride. He called the poor his brothers. We are brothers and sisters of one another, too, with the responsibilities that go along with that close relationship.

THE BATTLE ROYALE

Harold: The ceremony is only three days away, My Sweet. Don't you think we ought to discuss our vows?

Judy: Of course, Dearest, I was just about to suggest it myself.

Harold: Two minds thinking as one! What bliss! But tell me, My Dove, what is that book you're reading?

Judy: *The Prophet* by Kahlil Gibran. It's very inspiring. You should read it, Dear Heart.

Harold: I shall — at the first opportunity, Sugar Plum. Now about our vows . . .

Judy: I've written down a few things if you'd like to hear them.

Harold: I'd be enchanted, Love of My Life. Do read on!

Judy: 'Love has no other desire but to fulfil itself.'

Harold: I couldn't agree more, Fairest. Please continue.

Judy: 'But if you love and must needs have desires, let these be your desires:
  "To melt and be like a running brook that sings its melody to the night.
  To know the pain of too much tenderness."'

Harold: Poetic, to be sure, Rose Blossom. But do you think it's enough?

Judy: There's more, My Impatient One: 'Love one another, but make not a bond of love:
  "Let it rather be a moving sea between the shores of your souls."'

Harold: Inscrutable, Beloved. What are you trying to tell me?

Judy: That the oak tree and the cypress grow not in each other's shadow.

Harold: I see. Are you saying you want separate beds, Flower Bud? Is that it?

Judy: Of course not, Love Monkey. It's just that most marriage vows are quite restrictive. I feel we need some space to ourselves.

Harold: Oh, I agree. I do, indeed. But I think I'd prefer more traditional vows, Honey Dove.

Judy: I should have expected that, I suppose. Still, I rather hoped you'd join the New Age, Sugar Bun.

Harold: How so, My Kumquat? What's wrong with the traditional marriage vows?

Judy: The traditional vows are wonderful — *if* you happen to be a man.

Harold: As ever I am, Observant One. But am I hearing you say that you consider them sexist? Surely, they give women a fair shake.

Judy: Whatever gave you that idea, My Prince? Did you sleep through the women's liberation movement?

Harold: On the contrary. I'm all for women's lib. But enlighten me further, Moon Pie, for I fail to see the hitch in '. . . for richer or poorer; in sickness and in health . . . from this day forward as long as ye both shall live .'

Judy: Are you really blind then, Light of My Life? Or are you just trying to aggravate me? Anyone with half a brain knows that those old-fashioned vows have kept women in shackles and chains for centuries! I'm not going to be shackled to anyone!

Harold: Not even me, I take it. Am I correct, Passion Fruit?

Judy: I've got to be me, Love Bird. If you truly loved me, you wouldn't want it any other way.

Harold: So, just because I want to marry you, I'm guilty of standing in the way of your self-fulfilment. Forgive me, My One and Only, but it sounds as if you don't consider marriage a partnership built of mutual respect and trust.

Judy: Where do you get these ideas, My Dear Neanderthal? I do believe I'm seeing a completely different side of you. My friend, Marsha, was right. Talk of marriage and all men become jailers.

Harold: And all women prisoners — is that what you mean?

Judy: You're peevish, Love Bud. I guess the truth is bitter.

Harold: The truth? You're viewing marriage as a women's prison and men as jailors, Sweet Pea. I certainly never suggested any such thing.

Judy: Marsha had the same trouble with David before they were married.

Harold: David? But Marsha is married to John, My Forgetful Darling.

Judy: You're so-o rational, Angel Pie. Marsha married John after breaking up with David.

Harold: I know I'm going to regret this, Joy of Joys, but why oh why did Marsha break up with David? Had it anything to do with the subject under discussion?

Judy: Stupidity is not a virtue, My Delight. Try to stay with the conversation. Marsha dumped David because he was pig-headed enough to insist on traditional vows at their wedding.

Harold: The swine! But nothing like that is going to happen to us, is it, My Little Peach?

Judy: Perish the thought, *Mi Amora!* I'm certain that this chat has cleared up any potential misunderstandings. Wouldn't you agree?

Harold: Wholeheartedly, Betrothed. May I see that book you're reading?

Judy: I knew you'd be supportive, My Pet. I've underlined a few sections for you. I would memorize them if I were you. One gets so nervous during a wedding ceremony, I'm told.

'The most important thing a father can do for his children is to love their mother.'
Theodore Hesburgh

African children, traditionally brought up in large, extended families. In the West, families have either shrunk or have broken down completely. The full effect this has on children is still being measured.

The family is serious business as far as God is concerned. He set it up, he has a vested interest in its success, and he uses it to illustrate what our relationships should be like.

The Christian church has traditionally viewed marriage as a sacrament, 'an outward and visible sign of an inward and spiritual grace,' according to the definition of Augustine. It's more than a matter of convenience; it has a deeper spiritual quality about it.

That spiritual quality comes in part from the sexual relationship between a husband and wife. The Bible says that the body is a *temple* for God's Holy Spirit. A sexual relationship between two 'temples' is a spiritual union, creating from two separate individuals a single person. Any children resulting from this union are, in a very real sense, God's with the parents as caretakers. Parenthood should be approached with reverence, since

mothers and fathers are accountable to God for the way they care for the charges entrusted to them.

Christians also recognize that each individual human being is part of the human family. As children of the same heavenly Father, we are absolutely and undeniably connected with one another. If God is our father, then we are all brothers and sisters, and so must consider every other person we meet as one to whom we owe the same kind of love and respect that we do to our own blood-relations.

WHY FAMILIES?

The family is important to God because relationships are important to God. God wants to have a close relationship with us; he wants us to live in a close relationship with him and with others.

Nothing is worth anything until it

OLD AGE: THE LAST FRONTIER

The New Age is no place for old-timers.

The elderly were at one time considered important, valuable, and worthy of respect for no other reason than that they had weathered the storms of life. Society ascribed status to them on the basis of their age.

Now, the old are required to deny their age and at least *think* young even if they can't act young. The elderly are required to contribute something of value to society as they move into their last years — even if it's just babysitting our children or washing our dishes. To maintain status in the New Age, a person must continually *achieve*.

The inability of many old people to achieve any kind of status for themselves because of uncooperative bodies, forgetful minds, or broken spirits places them at odds with the rest of society.

Instead of finding a place for aged parents and grandparents in our hearts and lives, we are more likely to find a place for them in retirement villages, nursing homes, mental hospitals, or apartments of their own where they won't disturb our tight little sub-nuclear families.

For the aged are ever-present reminders of who we are and premonitions of what we will be. Medical science has guaranteed that more of us will live longer, but can we cope with the despair of loneliness, the pain of infirmity, the challenge of age-enforced poverty?

Depending on the attitudes of the family, friends and society, old age can bring respect and security or loneliness and despair.

touches another person. Everything we do is, ultimately, defined in the context of relationships. And relationships exist at their most fundamental level within the family. This is where it all starts.

Some pilgrims may be disappointed because the *Guide* has not indicated whether it is right or wrong to live in a commune, have a child out of wedlock, stay at home with small children or pursue a career, or send an aging parent to live in a nursing home.

The Christian definition of marriage covers many contingencies, respects many cultural traditions, and recognizes many individual needs and inclinations. The early Christians lived in family units *and* communally as well. Some of the early followers of Jesus were single and some were married. The Bible contains advice and help for people in any number of family situations.

No matter what form they may take, *all* marriage and family situations (and for that matter, all lifestyle situations) must be brought into a relationship with God. If they cannot, then something is fundamentally wrong with them, and they need to be changed. If they cannot be changed they must be abandoned.

Be absolutely certain that God won't be changing any of *his* ideas, visions, or expectations for marriage and the family. Remember, he is a cosmic constant. He is here for the duration.

When human relationships don't measure up to his standards, it is not God's fault. It's the fault of those who are involved in them. God gives purpose and vitality to the family, as he does to life itself. A family lacking vitality, love, or respect for one another, should look to the Source for help.

Will there be disappointment? Yes. Will there be problems? Yes. Will there be tragedy? Alienation? Divorce? Yes, yes, yes.

The difference is that all these outcomes will be recognized for what they are — the unwillingness or the inability of individuals to have the kind of relationships God wants them to have. Defeat in the family will not be rationalized or idealized as the norm, or assigned to an inevitability of life. People will admit their defeats, and will seek reconciliation — all in relation to God.

The wonder is that those families and marriages actively looking for God's help will be blessed, many times over. Not necessarily in any material sense, but certainly spiritually. God has a special place for the family and has promised to give to those who give to each other and to him. Any family that holds God at its heart is part of God's family.

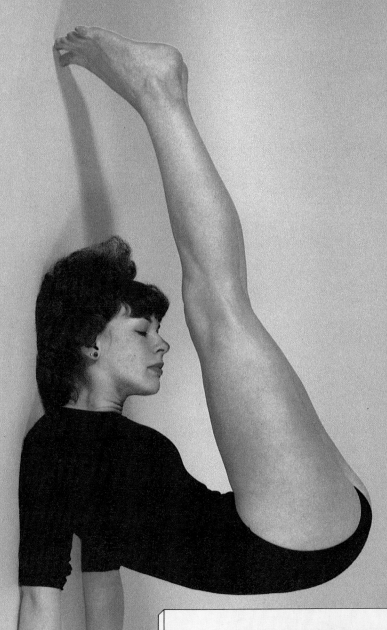

TOUR FOUR

TAKE ONE HUMAN

THE BODY

The human body presents a bit of a problem in the New Age. There are questions: is the body a *barrier* to true self-fulfilment, or is it actually *the road* to self-fulfilment? Is the body to be minimized in importance (as the ascetics have believed) or should it be maximized?

At any rate, we are finding that we must create new ways to relate to our bodies. Friend or foe, there is much greater emphasis on the importance of the body in the New Age. We think about bodies a great deal — some of us are absolutely preoccupied with them: how they move, how they look, how they function, what their limits are.

It can be argued that we are taking better care of them than ever before. We try not to work them so hard, give them the nourishment they require, and fight their propensity for disease and decay. (It could also be argued that our average intake of pesticides, pollutants and harmful chemicals of all kinds is hurting our bodies as never before . . . And this is all very well for the First and Second Worlds, but what about the Third?

If nothing else, we Westerners can be assured that most of us can plan on having them around years longer than, say, our ancestors of a hundred years ago.

Everyone has a big theory about something that used to be pretty much taken for granted: how to live in and with the standard equipment of human existence — the body.

PUMPING IRON

Pumping iron: the discipline of lifting incredible amounts of weight ('iron') in a rhythmic, repetitive way ('pumping') with the goal of building muscle tissue in the body, according to a predetermined plan.

Body-building, always a favorite activity for a select group of body culturists, has been made recently and widely popular by Arnold Schwarzenegger, six-time Mr. Olympia and recipient of numerous other awards for his impressively organized body. 'No pain, no gain', claim iron-pumpers, who dedicate themselves to lifting more and ever more weight, adding repetitions over a period of time until their greased bodies resemble nothing so much as overinflated diving suits.

Not merely the domain of male body aesthetes, women, too, are entering the arena of body building. Says guru Schwarzenegger, 'When you feel secure enough with yourself, with your body, then you are really free to be feminine and beautiful, to be yourself.'

He encourages potential body-builders to realize that their minds and bodies are a single unit. Don't treat your body as if it were a piece of luggage that you must carry with you throughout life, says Arnold. 'Your body and mind are one: two parts of a whole. They are you. Mind and

The New Age fascination with the body is exemplified — even parodied — by iron pumpers, on an endless quest for more developed muscles.

body cannot and should not be separated.'

RUNNING

Once considered mere child's play, running is now an activity performed by adults who utilize the long-distance run as a means to gain physical fitness.

As summarized by Jim Fixx (who wrote *The Complete Book of Running* and, sadly, was recently the victim of a heart attack — while running) the exercise of running fulfils a number of needs (need fulfilment, as you will remember, is the hallmark of any New Age movement):

1. The need for movement — considered an inborn physiological need.

2. The need for self-assertion — provides a socially acceptable means through which to express competitiveness.

3. The need for alternations of stress and relaxation — physical activity can alleviate mental stress.

4. The need for mastery over ourselves — assumes a latent need in each person to struggle for and against . . . something.

5. The need to indulge ourselves — running can be an antidote to overeating and overdrinking, thereby allowing overindulgence to go undetected.

6. The need to play — even though running has all these therapeutic effects, the element of recreation is not lost.

7. The need to lose ourselves in something greater than ourselves — the occasional euphoria obtained through strenuous running translates the individual into an other-world state.

8. The need to meditate — runners are removed from the stimuli (phone, television, etc.) that intrude on their thoughts.

9. The need to live to our own rhythms — running is done at one's own pace, in one's own time.

Jogging, unlike crazes like skateboarding, roller disco and the Rubik's Cube, seems to be here to stay, for a while at least. Thousands more people enter for the London and New York Marathons than are actually chosen to participate.

'Running ... can be a way of discovering our larger selves. I am finding that average people as well as superstars touch spiritual elements when they least expect it.'
Mike Spino

ANOREXIA NERVOSA

Medical texts of the last hundred years or so have reported cases of individuals who simply refuse to eat, thereby putting themselves at severe physiological risk. While still uncommon, the problem is much more prevalent today than it ever was before. It seems that there are more and more people (mostly young women) who have taken dieting a

---

Aerobics: a variety of exercises that stimulate heart and lung activity for a sustained period of time, thereby producing beneficial changes in the body.

Developed by Kenneth H. Cooper, MD, as a fitness program for the United States Air Force, aerobic exercise has

AEROBICS

caught on like wildfire. The variety of exercises include aerobic-quality walking, jogging, running, biking, swimming, calisthenics, dancing, weight-training, stair-climbing — any kind of movement done hard and long enough to give

the heart and lungs a good workout.

Aerobics has spawned a tremendous fashion industry, too. Tights and leotards, leg warmers, ballet slippers, athletic shoes, sweat bands and warm-up suits are all

potentially part of the wardrobe of the aerobic fitness buff. Or they are equally attractive to posers who want to dress 'physically fit' even if they aren't.

WHAT YOU EAT, YOU ARE

Everyone who is taking in nourishment is on a diet, in the strictest sense of the word. But it often seems that nearly everyone is on some kind of special diet, designed to achieve some purpose for the body.

Been on a good diet lately? There are plenty available, depending on what you're trying to accomplish, or what your weaknesses are. There's the Drinking Man's Diet, the New Mother's Diet, the Star Athlete's Diet, the Gourmet Diet, the Tennis Player's Diet, the Eat to Win Diet, and the Jet-Lag Diet.

You may choose the Low-Cal, Low-Sodium, Low-Cholesterol, Low-Sugar, Low-Fat (probably low-fun, too) Diet; the Anti-Breast-Cancer Diet; the Macrobiotic Diet; the Preconception Gender Diet; the Candy-Lover's Diet; the Fat-Disintegrator Diet; the Weight-Loss-During-Sex Diet; the Never-Say-Diet diet.

Or if those aren't to your taste, how about the I Love America Diet; the Bronx Diet; the Cambridge Diet; the California Diet; or the Swedish Diet?

Some diets promote the adage that you are what you eat; others that thin is in (never that fat's where it's at); that your life will change when the weight of your body changes; that life-threatening medical conditions can be held at bay when proper nutrition is summoned to the rescue.

With all the hoopla around diets, quite a number of former fatties have caught on to the fact that there is a lot of money to be made in the diet-book game. It's easy for book-sales-counting to take over from calorie-counting.

It seems that everyone — not just the diet gurus — has a theory about what is a proper diet. Actually *eating* properly is always a challenge, of course. But diet-consciousness exists as a subset to self-consciousness in the New Age.

Links between eating refined foods and various diseases have persuaded many people to switch to diets that are high in fiber and free from preservatives.

bit too far. They see the beautiful, happy, ultra-skinny fashion models and decide that being skinny is their salvation (since it makes one so beautiful and happy) and set about the task of making sure they get gaunt.

Most stop before any real physical damage is done. They get hungry and succumb, they lose their resolve, or lose the fat and let it go at that. But a few don't know when to quit, and they continue to starve themselves — sometimes to death.

Anorexia nervosa is a peculiarly tragic result of the belief that *You Are How You Look*.

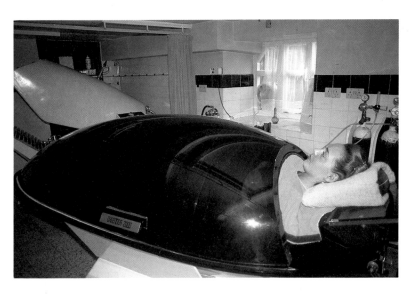

OBESITY

Obesity is, in most cases, a pretty high-class problem. We get to be obese because we have plenty of food, because in most cases overweight is caused by over-consumption.

In societies where there is plenty of hard work for everyone and very little food to fuel the body, a plump physique is a sign of wealth and prosperity. In Western societies, where food is so available, and fatness so likely, the slim body is admired. It seems that we tend to idealize the body type that is the least likely to be obtained by the largest majority of the population.

The prevailing opinion is that obesity is not fashionable. Fat bodies are not beautiful bodies, and are unequipped to handle the challenge of the New Age.

DISABLED OR DIFFERENTLY ABLED?

Disability: a condition that restricts or limits — especially a physical condition that puts one at a disadvantage in relation to others.

Ironically, the definitions themselves have proven the biggest barrier to hundreds of thousands of people all over the world whose bodies don't look, work, or respond in a way that is considered normal. Only recently Chicago repealed its 'ugly' law: a statute stating that no one 'diseased, maimed, mutilated or in any way deformed so as to be an unsightly or disgusting object' may step out in public.

Increasingly, though, the emphasis is away from what the disabled cannot do, and toward what they *can* do — which is often much more than is popularly thought. This positive outlook is quickly leading to the obsolescence of words like 'cripple,' 'retarded,' 'idiot,' 'lame,' and 'blind' and an increased usage of such words as 'exceptional,' 'differently abled,' 'unsighted,' and so on.

Bruce, a quadriplegic
'I have my ups and downs, but I'm leading a life. That's the important thing. I'm not warehoused in some institution. I'm not a vegetable that needs to be watered every two days. I'm leading a life.'

Virginia, disabled by polio
'I just don't understand the

If you don't want to reduce your diet, there's always the weight-reducing machine. According to one estimate, the populations of the United States and Canada are approximately 100,000 tons overweight.

NEW PORTABLE WEIGHT-REDUCING MACHINE!

discrimination. I guess it all boils down to America playing up the body. If you don't look like Tom Terrific or Barbara Body, you're an outcast. It's sort of like we're all carbon copies. All the black guys have a certain look, all the white girls have a certain look, all the white guys have a certain look. If you look different or act different, you should be shunned. We've got to say to people, "Hey, here we are. We're not like everybody else. We're here, though. Whether you like it or not, we're here. You're going to have to learn to live with us."'

Tanya, disabled by rheumatoid arthritis

'I have accepted my disability. I can't say I don't get angry when I drop something on the floor and can't pick it up. But I don't let anger overtake me. I'm not going to paint the picture of the super crip. Some people make out that they're the super crip and it's wonderful to be disabled. Well, that's going overboard the other way. It's never wonderful to be disabled. But you can still be a whole person. You can still be a happy person.'

ADDICTION

Addiction: a state of 'periodic or chronic intoxication produced by the repeated consumption of a natural or synthetic drug for which one has an overpowering desire or need to continue to take . . .' World Health Organization.

'A person should be considered addicted when an overpowering, repetitive, excessive need exists for some substance, object, feeling, act, milieu, or personal interaction at any cost, along with a denial of the destructive consequences to one's physical, emotional, and social well-being and, in some instances, to economic survival.' Dr Lawrence J. Hatterer, *The Pleasure Addicts*

Addiction is most generally a word used in connection with certain chemical dependencies: tobacco, caffeine, alcohol, or certain pharmaceuticals. But it may also be applied to other activities, as in 'addicted to his job' (workaholic); 'crazy for the horses' (gambling addiction); or 'simply must have it' (compulsive need to spend money).

ALCOHOLISM

Drunkenness used to be considered an act of will and therefore a sin. This sort of moralistic judgmentalism is strictly passé in the New Age. Now there is no such animal as a drunk; we have 'problem drinkers' who may become alcoholics. Alcoholism is an illness now, not a sin; alcoholics are sick, sufferers of a debilitating disease.

After the enforced prohibition of all alcoholic beverages in the United States failed so miserably (in the 1920s and 30s), it was common to hear people say to anyone wanting to control the availability of alcohol, 'You can't legislate morality; Prohibition proved that.'

Ironically, now that drinking is no longer a *moral issue*, and alcoholism has been established as a disease, thereby making it a *health issue*, there is a revived public interest in personal drinking habits. Movements have started to raise the legal drinking age, to restrict alcohol advertising, to establish stricter penalties for driving while intoxicated, and to educate the public about the dangers of drinking — not in the name of morality, but in the interest of public health.

'No thanks, I don't drink,' is becoming an increasingly acceptable — even admired — reply when alcohol is being offered.

NICOTINE

Nicotine: 'An extremely poisonous alkaloid found in tobacco leaves' (from Jacques Nicot, French diplomat, who introduced tobacco into France c1560).

Nicotine is the substance in tobacco smoke and juice that produces a narcotic effect. This narcotic can be easily obtained by drawing air through a lit cigarette, cigar, or tobacco-filled pipe, by inhaling pulverized tobacco, or by allowing saliva to work on flaked tobacco placed in the mouth. In these ways, the chemical substances in tobacco are assimilated into the body.

The pattern of tobacco addiction occurs basically like this: an individual begins smoking (or dipping snuff, or chewing tobacco) some time during the adolescent period in order to imitate adulthood; later, the same individual seeks to extinguish the acquired behavior — again in an effort to look like an adult.

DRUGS

Drugs: any number of consciousness-altering chemical preparations; often psychologically and/or physically addicting; usually illegal, with controlled distribution.

Drug-use hit a peak of sorts in the 1960s and 70s, when vast numbers of young people, especially, experimented with drugs, goaded on by gurus like Ken Kesey and Timothy Leary, inspired by trendsetters like the

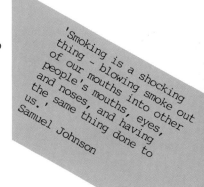

'Smoking is a shocking thing — blowing smoke out of our mouths into other people's mouths, eyes, and noses, and having the same thing done to us.' Samuel Johnson

'If God can be found through the medium of any drug, God is not worthy of being God.'
Meher Baba

A researcher uses ultraviolet light on DNA during cancer research work. While medical science has dramatically changed the quality of life in the 20th century, it has also raised a host of thorny issues.

Beatles, and encouraged by their friends.

The young of the 1960s and 70s are middle-aged now, and many of them continue to use illegal, consciousness-altering drugs (if less zealously) while others have switched to the legal drugs, mostly alcohol.

The popularity of a particular drug waxes and wanes: for a while it's marijuana or hash; then LSD and mescaline are the rage; heroin always has its following; cocaine is the preferred means of destruction for today's young, upwardly mobile urban professionals.

The fact is that most of us are 'on' some drug, whether it's one of the more exotic types mentioned above, or alcohol, nicotine, caffeine, or the eminently respectable sugar-high.

What makes us so devoted to our mind-altering pick-me-ups? The power of curiosity — at least at the initial stages of drug use — would be hard to overestimate. Especially in adolescents and those who have an adventurous streak, curiosity plays a big role in deciding to take drugs. The social milieu of one's time is also a deciding factor. The mere availability of a particular drug in a particular social setting will decide, in large part, its usage. If it's on hand, it's likely to be tried; if it's out of reach, only the more determined will seek it out.

On a less practical level, those with a strong taste for The Other, with a desire to expand their experiences and their consciousness, or obtain a religious experience, will often look to drugs to aid them in their journey. The negative side of that interest is a strong desire to escape from one's reality. This is often used to explain the extremely high usage in urban ghettos of heroin: a drug with a great capacity to facilitate mental escape when there is something truly awful to run from.

WISE AND FOOLISH TECHNOLOGY

'Physicists have now known sin,' is what Robert Oppenheimer, father of the atomic bomb, is reported to have said when the first experimental nuclear explosion took place. The belief he challenged is that there is no sin in science. It used to be said that science deals with facts and facts only, and facts, as we all know, are strictly amoral.

But we live in a world of moral decisions and values. David Hume, an eighteenth-century philosopher, described the tension between what *is* and what *ought* to be (the Is-Ought dichotomy) as the 'naturalistic fallacy.' He called for an end to the kind of thinking that maintains: if it's possible, then let us by all means proceed with it.

Hume put forth the belief that there is an unbridgeable gap between what is and what ought to be, science dealing with what is (the facts of the physical universe) and ethics considering what ought to be (values which can guide human activity).

If wisdom exists, it is the result of knowledge tempered by judgment, and the search for wisdom is one that constantly compares what *is* happening with what *ought* to be happening.

An anxious pilgrim might wonder what any of these interesting philosophical nuggets have to do with

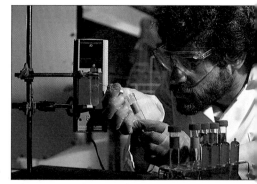

FRONT-LINE TECHNIQUES

What are the major, earth-shaking technological changes that demand our ethical evaluation?

Genetic engineering

Also called 'participatory evolution,' it began with artificial insemination and will likely end with bioengineered or technologically-designed parahumans. Genetic engineering is nothing less than the ability to affect our own biological evolution.

Recombinent DNA

'Gene-splicing.' This involves tinkering with the double helix of DNA in the hope of understanding, regulating, and changing genetic structure, and hence life.

Genetic Screening

The evaluation of a potential pregnancy or a pregnancy-in-progress with a view toward uncovering and possibly correcting or avoiding any genetic abnormalities that would pose risks to parents or child.

Fetal Research It is now possible to use the healthy tissue of an aborted fetus or a viable in-utero fetus for scientific experimentation.

Cloning Once a joke, no one's laughing now. Apparently, scientists have within their grasp the capabilities of asexual reproduction of human beings, using cells from the 'parent' to produce *exact* duplicates — carbon copies of the original.

Physical Intervention in the Brain

Electroshock, electrostimulation and psychosurgery can manipulate the way humans behave. Although much of the early research into brain functions was done with unwilling or unknowing subjects (criminals, mental patients, social 'undesireables'), psychosurgery is becoming more common and accepted as treatment

for many mental and physical disorders.

Birth Control The age-old sexual equation: *man+woman=child* is no longer a mathematical certainty. There are now available any number of means by which a sexually active individual can be protected from the possibility of parenthood. The Pill, the 'morning after' pill, sterilization and abortion are the more controversial methods.

Euthanasia Proponents call it the right to die; opponents call it murder. Deciding not to use extraordinary or heroic measures to preserve a life is called passive euthanasia; deciding to deliberately end a life when the patient is suffering from an irremedial condition is called active euthanasia. Both are almost universally illegal.

Transplants Always a controversial topic (especially when it comes to deciding whether a donor is *dead enough* to remove an organ that can be transplanted to the recipient, but *alive enough* for that organ to be viable) it is again becoming a topic of conversation at dinner, now that it appears possible to place animal parts in human bodies.

Test Tube Fertilization

The tricky business of uniting egg and sperm (it's the lack of ability to perform this feat that causes so much infertility in humans) can now be performed in a laboratory, in an artificial womb. Once the fertilized egg is well on its way to becoming a viable fetus (after a few days), then it can be placed in the uterus of the mother, who will take over from there, carrying it until birth.

Artificial Insemination

The big noise concerns couples in which the wife is unable to bear children. A surrogate mother is inseminated with the husband's sperm; she carries the child to term, then gives the newborn child to the couple who commissioned the birth. Problems arise when the surrogate decides (as she often does) that she wants to keep *her* baby. Now what?

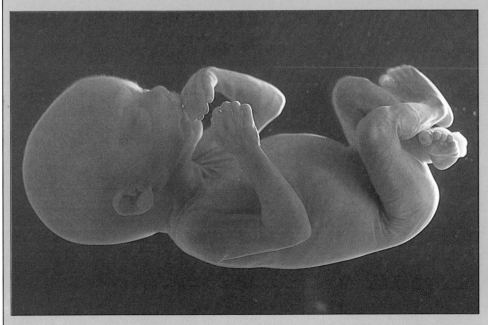

Many front-line medical techniques focus on the very beginnings of human life. Is it right to use the human fetus in scientific experimentation? When does human life start to be human life? This fetus is twelve weeks old.

the present tour: that is, the body.

In the case of the body, as we have already noted on our tour of the family, our scientific knowledge and technology are running way ahead of our social systems and our individual ability to handle that technology. Nowhere is this more evident than in the field of biogenetics. It seems that we daily gain access to procedures (what *is*) without having the vaguest idea what to do with them (what *ought* to be).

The need to cope with the disparity between technology and human values is a primary concern of the New Age. In the New Age we reject the idea that we must endorse any scientific advancement merely because it exists.

We reserve the right to assess it in light of human values and ascertain its worth on that basis.

The method by which we make the judgment will probably fall in one of two schools of thought that are currently popular:

● **Proportionate Good School:** Joseph Fletcher, a leading proponent, holds that an act 'acquires its value because it happens to help persons (thus being good), or to hurt persons (thus being bad).' This way of thinking is also called situation ethics, and it maintains that certain ends justify certain means, and that sometimes the good of an individual can be morally sacrificed when the proportionate good to society is great.

ACUPUNCTURE

1971 was a big year for Ping-Pong. The United States visited China to participate in cultural exchange Ping-Pong games. The game got a boost in popularity and the Americans learned humility at the hands of Oriental paddle masters. They also returned with stories about something much more exciting than lightning-quick diving backhand smashes: acupuncture.

Not wanting to be humiliated on yet another front, Western doctors, scientists, and interested cultural observers were almost unanimous in their rejection of 'Eastern quackery.' 'They won't fool us,' said the MD's and PhDs. 'We don't buy it!'

But certain of Hollywood's luminaries loved the idea. Zsa Zsa Gabor, Merv Griffin and Lorne Greene, among others, got needled and all sang the praises of the 'new' cure — which, as it turns out, is about 5,000 years old.

Perhaps it's the language that's so hard for Westerners to latch onto.

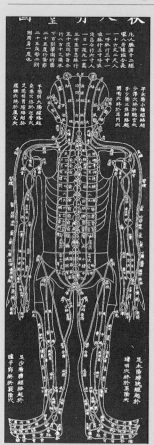

You see, the *Yin* and *Yang* must be brought into balance to effect healing. The Life Force — *Ch'i* (also spelt *Tschi'i* or *Qi*) — travels through special pipelines called meridians. *Ch'i*, of course, is controlled by the mysterious organ Triple Warmer. These meridians, called *Ching*, correspond with the energy mutations of the *Tsang Fu* (for that, read 'organs'). All this is pretty hard for a head-and-shoulders-knees-and-toes Western medical doctor to understand.

Still, if the language is hard to understand, the results are equally hard to deny. Centuries of well-documented cases in China, Japan and Korea attest to the power of acupuncture to treat such diverse ailments as acne, anaemia, diabetes, colitis, hemorrhoids, hypertension, migraine headaches, rheumatism, schizophrenia, vertigo, anaemia (again),

A map of the body, as seen by acupuncturists.

bronchitis, encephalitis and glaucoma . . . not to mention its prodigious benefits as an anesthetic for surgical use. And if one is reluctant to believe those proofs, acupuncture's increasingly wide-spread use in the United States, Britain, France, Russia and other Western countries has produced a parallel body of literature documenting impressive results.

The New Age, ever quick to rediscover an old process (especially if it flies in the face of accepted science and contemporary technology) made room for the prickly Oriental import. The result? We now have major universities and medical centers sponsoring acupuncture clinics and training, a certain tolerance of Oriental practitioners in the United States, and medical exchange programs between the West and China, whereby Western physicians are becoming educated in the ancient art of acupuncture.

AURA-READING

Aura: an etheric atmosphere, or electromagnetic color field thought to surround all living things.

An aura reader in New York claims the ability to determine whether someone is an alcoholic or heavy drug user simply by examining the shades of the individual's aura. A psychic in California claims to have successfully treated arthritis, cystitis, and liver disease by reading the sufferer's aura and then applying the correct type of massage.

An aura reader who calls himself 'The Man with Kaleidoscope Eyes' claims to know the most intimate details of a stranger's life because he can discern personality traits, habits, and even past, present and future experiences by analyzing the auric envelope.

This, for those who have the knack, is not terribly difficult since, as luck would have it, auras conform quite religiously to idiomatic and stereotypic interpretations. For example, expressions such as, 'green with envy' or 'red with rage', as well as 'black-hearted', 'in the pink' and 'feeling blue' take a literal turn in the presence of aura readers, as the shades of one's aura tend to signify exactly what one might expect they would.

Those with the gift for reading auras are generally at a loss to explain why they are able to do what they do, or how another person might cultivate the ability (aside from depositing large amounts of cash in the psychic's secret Swiss bank account, which may not help, but certainly couldn't hurt). Aura readers insist that auras cannot be ignored as diagnostic tools for analyzing a patient's physical complaints, emotional difficulties, mental problems, or spiritual concerns. The aura, it seems, tells all.

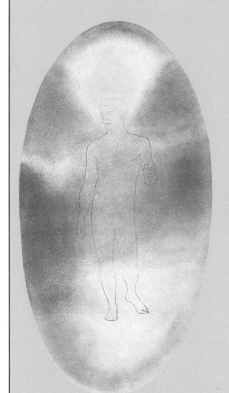

Auras are said to vary according to the person's character, mood and health. This depiction of an aura shows a calm, scientific man.

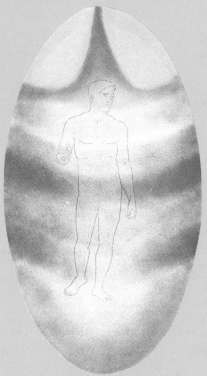

The aura of an intelligent man.

The aura of a man who is in love.

● **Prohibitionist School:** Currently being defended by Paul Ramsey, this school of thought maintains that there are things that can be done that should not be done; there are things that can be known that should not be known — because they pose such serious, profound, and unresolveable ethical problems for individuals and society. In other words, there are scientific taboos. Human life is sacred, and its value cannot be weighed against any greater public good.

ROLFING

Rolfing is an approach to the personality through the myfascial colagen components of the physical body.

Named after its developer, Ida Rolf, rolfing is a ten-hour cycle of deep manual 'intervention' (massage and manipulation) that is designed to reorient the body so that it is in tune with the earth's gravity field, thereby restoring balance and equilibrium.

The exact nature of the massage is unclear (no one at the *Guide* has been rolfed and rolfers don't like to say too much about what actually happens), but it is sometimes called 'elbowing' (now, *that's* a clue), and is sometimes painful — although the official doctrine of rolfing attributes such pain to the subject's unwillingness to change.

In aligning the myfascial structure (connective tissue system) of the body, each part of the body is brought to the place where it anatomically belongs, thereby establishing a new movement pattern.

This process is called the Integration of Human Structures. Says Dr Rolf: 'This is the gospel of rolfing: when the body gets working appropriately, the force of gravity can flow through. Then, spontaneously, the body heals itself.'

So does the soul, apparently. Since misalignment in the body may be the result of emotional trauma and psychological problems as well as physical abnormalities, the correction of the body can force the person being rolfed to confront past experiences with a view toward health and wholeness.

YOGA

Yoga: a system of physical and mental self-improvement, emphasizing union of the body, mind and spirit.

There are many kinds of yoga, among them Jnana Yoga (with an emphasis on the intellect); Bhakti Yoga (salvation through love); Karma Yoga (yoga of action); Mantra Yoga (sound and vibration — the yoga of Transcendental Meditation and the Hare Krishnas); and the popular Hatha Yoga.

Hatha is the yoga of physical culture, combining body stretching and regulated breathing to produce flexibility, health and vitality. Toward this end it employs rhythmic exercises, isometrics, calisthenics, and dance movements. A very subtle, graceful exercise, it is the antithesis of more strenuous types of exercises like pumping iron or aerobics, as it brings the body into complex formations that stretch unused muscles, ligaments and tendons.

Many Eastern teachers put Hatha Yoga at the bottom of the Yoga pile, since it stresses the body so much. More advanced yogas, while conceding that the body should be in perfect condition to achieve a perfect spiritual state, believe that the body is a mere vessel for the soul, or self, and therefore of little consequence.

BODY LANGUAGE

Body language: any non-reflexive or reflexive movement of a part, or all of the body, used by a person to communicate an emotional message to the outside world.

One interesting outgrowth of a

holistic understanding of life (that the mind, body and spirit are part of a unified whole) is the belief that human beings are constantly transmitting mental and emotional messages through their bodies: postures, gestures and expressions.

Body language has to do with interpreting the way you hold your arms, the amount of personal space you demand, the tilt of your head, the way your legs are crossed, how you twitch your nose, and so on down to your toes. It's a field day for the amateur, and there's nothing as aggravating as being told: 'I know you *say* you love me, but your body says no!' As the Chinese proverb states: 'Beware of the man whose stomach doesn't move when he laughs.'

CIRCADIAN RHYTHMS

Circadian rhythms are the body's inherent daily rhythms. Now, let's not get confused. Circadian rhythms are not bio-rhythms. Bio-rhythms are very popular at present. You can get charts and computer programs that tell what your bio-rhythms are. They assume that your rhythm began on the day of birth, manifests itself in life's ups and downs, and eventually dictates the day of death.

All this isn't scientifically proven or especially well documented, but that doesn't decrease its popularity much.

More legitimate is the work being done in chronobiology — the study of living organisms with respect to time. What has been known to be true about plants for generations (such as that some bloom once a year, some every two years, and one Japanese variety every 120 years!) is now known to be true about humans. No, humans don't bloom; but they do lots of other things just as predictably and with the same kind of precise periodicity.

By simply logging such phenomena as body temperature, blood pressure, heart rate and sleep patterns in the course of a 24-hour period, one's body rhythms can be discerned. Circadian rhythms, or 'day rhythms,' also hold for the human race generally. By noting the time at which most natural births, deaths, industrial accidents and the like occur in the human population, the broader rhythm of life can be seen.

Interest lies in helping people determine their peak working time (greater efficiency) and in dealing with such phenomena as jet lag, which occurs when you are suddenly dislocated in time, causing a violent intrusion in your circadian rhythm.

BIOFEEDBACK

It was once thought that involuntary body processes, such as the pressure with which the blood was pumped by the heart, the rate of flow through the veins and arteries, the temperature of the body, and so on, were beyond the control of the individual. They were involuntary states of the body. It is now known that these 'involuntary' processes *can* be controlled, and the way to do it is to provide the individual with some means by which those processes can be read — fed back in a form he or she can see. The

A gura is wired up to a biofeedback machine to show that he can affect his blood pressure, body temperature, and other 'involuntary' processes.

person can then be trained to do whatever it is that needs to be done to bring these processes under control.

Toward this end, the body can be hooked up to machines that indicate brain activity, skin responses, muscle tension, blood pressure, or skin temperature. Using EEGs, ESR, EMPs and all the rest, subjects can learn how to produce a beneficial effect for him or herself by mentally manipulating their physical condition — all for the purpose of alleviating or curing any number of medical symptoms and conditions. Headaches, flaccid muscles, insomnia, anxiety, depression, stress, or high blood pressure — they can all be controlled.

That's the medical approach. There is also a more mystical approach to biofeedback. Acknowledging its roots in the East (you know — lying on a bed of nails, walking on fire — that sort of thing), a yogi-type application can be given to the biofeedback procedure.

By utilizing biofeedback, the subject may achieve self-control over his or her most basic body processes, thereby gaining increased self-knowledge. Through the use of guided imagery and meditation, alpha rhythms may be produced (these constitute a desired state of electrical activity in the brain that produces calm and detached awareness). This leads to higher awareness; higher states of consciousness.

Remember the levels of consciousness in Transcendental Meditation? It's much the same here. It is said that there are nine levels of consciousness (see box).

'I'm a practicing hetero-sexual ... but bisexuality immediately doubles your chances for a date on Saturday night.'
Woody Allen

'No woman can call herself free who does not own and control her body. No woman can call herself free until she can choose consciously whether she will or will not be a mother.'
Margaret Sanger

THE SEXUAL REVOLUTION: WHO WON?

The Sexual Revolution of the 1960s and 70s is over. It is now a task for the 1980s and 90s to figure out who won.

But first, as always, a brief rundown of what led to the event. Some say it was The Pill that caused the revolution, giving women the freedom to have sex without having children. Others say it was the fact that women started working alongside men in all types of jobs, hence having a chance to meet men other than their husbands (why is it always the woman's fault?). Still others attribute it to the affluence of that period, noting that when the economy is up, so is sex (the last example of this was the Roaring 20s, a time of unprecedented wealth and sexual activity).

The *Guide* is likely to place a great deal of responsibility with those who advocated fulfilment of the human potential, and promoted the quest for self-actualization. The notion that the self should be fulfilled — and to heck with those who think it shouldn't — encouraged a whole generation to reject repressive attitudes about sex that were keeping them from being and experiencing everything they could.

And so, after twenty-odd years of sexual licence and indulgence, the revolution is over. Maybe no one won. Maybe the war just fizzled out. However it may be, it's clear that there have been some casualties: legions suffering from the increased incidence of venereal disease, including the dreaded, as-yet-incureable herpes; millions of unwanted pregnancies that terminated in abortion or grudging parenthood (often single); impotence stemming from the escalated expectations of the

THE NINE LEVELS OF CONSCIOUSNESS

0 Deep Sleep	4 Meditation/	6 Creativity
1 Dreaming Sleep	Transcendental	7 Illumination/God
2 Hypnotic state	Consciousness	Consciousness
3 Waking and Waking	5 Lucid Awareness/	8 Cosmic Consciousness/
Sleep	Cosmic Consciousness	Unity

revolution (expectations to perform and to perform *expertly*); a soaring divorce rate resulting from the yawning gap between expectation and reality on the part of the partners; disillusionment because intimacy didn't come along with the one-night-stand; and exhaustion from the demands of gourmet sex, exotic and ever more spectacular means of sexual expression to refresh jaded appetites.

One of the more interesting outcomes of the sexual revolution is the new chastity, the new celibacy. In the 1960s and 70s sexual reformers and revolutionaries were giving the troops permission to have sex. Now they are giving permission *not* to have sex. People with no moral axe to grind reserve for themselves the right to say 'no' to casual liaisons and 'no' to exotic erotics.

Can it be that we have begun to believe what our mothers were telling us all along?

DYING: A PART OF LIFE

Oriented as it is toward treating symptoms and fighting disease, the medical establishment tends to take a dim view of dying. And why not? Patients with the audacity to die are

insulting to those who would like to see them live — indefinitely.

Practitioners of the healing arts are, and have always been, respected, worshipped even, by those who entrust their lives to them. Still, there comes a time for each individual to die, and it is this elementary observation that has rocked the medical establishment to the core. New Agers are no longer content to see the dying used as human guinea pigs for exotic cures and procedures; to prolong vital signs indefinitely by

This lady, born at the end of the 19th century, clearly seems to be enjoying life towards the end of the 20th. New Agers, with their emphasis on the physical, have a difficult time coming to terms with ageing and dying.

CARE FOR THE DYING

The hospice movement exists to serve the dying. In the Middle Ages, hospices were run by monks and nuns who provided care for the poor, the sick, and pious wayfarers. In the early 1960s, Cicely Saunders revived the hospice concept in England, seeking a way to alleviate the pain of terminally ill cancer patients.

Hospice care, in its entirety, includes hospital and home care for the dying, a bereavement program, and community and in-service education for care-givers. The goal of all these efforts is to allow the dying person to face death with dignity, to ease any physical discomfort, and to provide support for the family and friends.

THE NEW AGE WILL

The fear of having one's life prolonged longer than one would wish has led to the Living Will: a legal document that any person may prepare and execute while healthy, or at least in the final stages of a terminal illness. Typically, it reads like a Last Will and Testament, authorizing and admonishing health-care givers and family and friends to let the patient die naturally, relieving pain, but not employing heroic high-tech means of prolonging life when there is no hope that the life saved will be productive or self-sustaining in the future.

If the New Age advocates that humans can rise from the ashes of technology, it also advocates that they can pass from this life to whatever lies beyond with some degree of dignity.

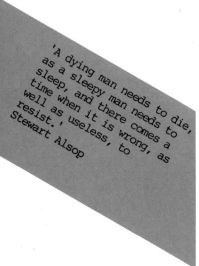

'A dying man needs to die, as a sleepy man needs to sleep, and there comes a time when it is wrong, as well as useless, to resist.'
Stewart Alsop

the use of respirators, ventilators, heart pumps and intravenous feedings; to dance around the inevitability of death in a hundred ways; and then finally to allow death to occur in the cold sterility of a hospital room bereft of the comfort of loved ones. Instead, New Age thinkers are working to rehumanize the dying process, recognizing it as a natural, inevitable part of life.

The *Guide* would like to be able to report that when death is inevitable, all health care professionals will conduct every bit of medical research safely, compassionately, and wisely; that technology will always be at the disposal of the patient — not the other way around; that patients of sound mind will be allowed to exercise control over their own care and treatment; that society in general will show itself devoted to the humane care of the sick and dying.

But, alas, this is not the case. The movement to humanize dying is certainly gaining momentum, but technology is still worshipped for its own sake, and death is still denied. It's clear that we still have a long way to go.

It was Elisabeth Kubler-Ross who opened the eyes of many, identifying the stages of dying, which are:

1. Denial and Isolation: 'No, not me; it cannot be true.'
2. Anger: 'Why me?'
3. Bargaining: 'If only I could live another year, I would . . .'
4. Depression: 'Never mind.'
5. Acceptance: 'I hope for life, but I can face death.'

Kubler-Ross has shown us that dying is normal, that those who are dying share many of the same reactions to their impending death, and that when we understand these reactions we can better help the dying and those who will still live.

THE END?

Death: the permanent end of all life. That's the kind of definition a naturalist would give. The naturalist believes that the life we live in this body on this planet, the life that begins at birth and ends at death, is all there is. The End. There is nothing before, and certainly nothing after.

Actually, that's a little hard for most people to accept. The supernaturalist point of view is more palatable. It holds that there is some kind of existence beyond this one: pre-existence, post-existence and/or spiritual existence in some form. Most people are supernaturalists when it comes to death.

We tend to be fascinated by the possibility that we existed in some way — spiritually or physically — before we were born into this life, and that our death will be merely a transition from this existence to some other plane of being. We like the idea that we are evolving, moving on to bigger and better things.

We have an intuitive sense about all this, which is often encouraged by phenomena that seem to point to pre- and post-life experiences: remembrances of past lives recalled under hypnosis; dreams and visions; unexplainable knowledge (possibly obtained in a past life) and life-after-death accounts of those who have

A funeral takes place in Africa. What happens when we die? While many Westerners have abandoned traditional Christian faith, life after death is still a strongly-held belief.

been pronounced clinically dead and are then resuscitated back to life.

The latter are of particular interest, since there is impressive agreement between those who have had an apparent after-death experience and then lived to tell about it. Even those with a naturalist bent are intrigued by the empirical data available and the consistency of experience.

NICE EARTH SUIT, KID

The *Guide* has pointed out earlier in the journey that Christian thought declares that human beings were and continue to be made in the image of God. Although no one has irrefutable proof of whether or not God has a body, it is known that God's Son (who is also God himself) had a body. We're talking here about Jesus Christ, who lived on this earth from 4 BC to AD 29 (or thereabouts).

It's really a very fascinating business to consider: that the Creator of the Universe lived inside an ordinary human body and pursued a mortal existence for thirty-three years — fantastic! The thought of such an incredible event is enough to get one thinking about one's own mortal body, its importance and the uses it might have — in the light of God becoming a human being.

For if, as we pointed out in our previous tours, human beings contain aspects of God, and if they are, like Jesus, children of a living God, we need go only one short step further to see that the billions of people now walking around on Planet Earth in regulation-issue bodies are quite a bit more than so many pounds of flesh and bone.

Think of it this way: man is a spirit, just like God. But we are also meant to live a physical existence — at least for a time. In order to do this, we are given an Earth Suit, especially designed by the Creator to house the human essence during our sojourn on Planet Earth.

This is not to say that bodies are not part and parcel of who and what we are. Quite the contrary. The *Guide* agrees with Arnold Schwarzenegger, who says the body is not a piece of luggage which we are doomed to drag with us through life. No, the Earth Suit is basic equipment for Planet Earth existence. If you don't have an Earth Suit, you can't live on Planet Earth. And living here is important; absolutely vital.

The human body at its best is agile, quick to react, efficient, smooth running, economical and adaptable. But who made it? And is there more to being human than the physical?

Now, some people obviously have really gorgeous Earth Suits. Victoria Principal has a great one; so does Daley Thompson. Little babies have cute, cuddly Earth Suits. Teenagers have uncooperative Earth Suits; so do most old people.

Some people have Earth Suits with kinks in them; they don't work as well as they might, they are weak, or they wear out quickly. The owners of these Earth Suits sometimes wish they had different ones. Sometimes they can be modified so that they are more functional and beautiful, but for the most part we live with the equipment we're given at birth and that we develop in the course of our lives.

Christians believe that people should take care of the Earth Suits. After all, they are given to us by a loving God, a powerful God, a God that says our bodies are temples (it stands to reason, you see, that if humans contain a spark of the divine, our bodies house that spark). It would be very poor form, indeed, to let one's Earth Suit disintegrate from lack of proper use, to become diseased or damaged because it was ill-fed or ill-used.

On the other hand, why devote *all* one's energy maintaining something of limited use? Remember that the Earth Suit is designed expressly for the purpose of living on Planet Earth. When we leave Planet Earth, we won't need it any more. It'll stay behind. There is reason to believe that the life beyond this one will require bodies; the Bible talks about getting new, improved bodies at some point later on. Certainly, anyone who's ever seen a dead body understands in no uncertain terms that when a person dies, Earth Suit and occupant part company; they quit sharing the same space. There is nothing more forlorn, more empty-looking, than an Earth Suit whose occupant has moved out.

Obviously, it's wrong to judge someone solely on the condition of his or her Earth Suit. To have prejudicial ideas about what constitutes an acceptable body and what doesn't, and then to determine a person's worth on that basis alone is unfair, and cruel as well.

The best choice? To understand that bodies are given by God. Sometimes it's hard to understand how a certain body could be, by any stretch of the imagination, considered to be in God's image. But that's what we are told. The extent to which you feel at home in your own body, and enjoy the bodies of others, is related to how completely you can accept the notion that God has big plans for everybody on Planet Earth.

TOUR FIVE

TAKE ONE HUMAN

THE ARTS

The *Guide* is cognizant of the fact
that each pilgrim will have his or her
own ideas about what constitutes
'art.' It may be ballet and classical
dance, Kabuki theater, Dire Strait's
latest album (the *Guide* is apt to agree
with you there), the huge Picasso
statue in Chicago's Daley Plaza,
graffiti on New York's subway trains,
Chagall's airplanes, or perhaps a
portrait of Elvis beautifully rendered
in day-glo colors on black velvet.

Well, as they say, there's no
accounting for taste — certainly not
the taste of our fellow travelers. But
whatever your definition of art,
Mozart or Madonna, Whistler or
Warhol, it is important to grasp some
sense of the importance of the arts in
the New Age.

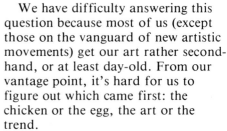

Many forms of modern artistic expression – sculpture, painting, architecture, modern music – can be criticized for being art for an elite club of artists and not for the ordinary person.

This is because the art of any age depicts, in a graphic, tangible, obvious way, the trends of the culture in which it exists. So we are faced with the age-old question: do the arts set the pace, or merely reflect the times? In other words, do the designs we see in our fashions, the movies we view at the theater, the music that plays on our radios, the architecture that fills our cities . . . does all this come to us simply as a reflection of where we already are, or does it bring us to a new place?

We have difficulty answering this question because most of us (except those on the vanguard of new artistic movements) get our art rather second-hand, or at least day-old. From our vantage point, it's hard for us to figure out which came first: the chicken or the egg, the art or the trend.

Take architecture, for example. Is the current penchant for exposed steel girders and poured concrete walls a result of elitist designers, architects, and engineers forcing us to live in glass houses, or are they merely giving the public what it wants — sleek, practical, awe-inspiring obelisks that reach to the heavens? Are the designers of our buildings presenting us with new possibilities, or are they merely complying with our cultural request for bigger, better, and higher office buildings, so that each city can out-skyscraper the next?

The *Guide* would suggest that on a practical level both are true: art leads and it also follows. This is because our world-wide culture is in varying stages of innovation and acceptance. An artist may believe that her dances are reflecting the mood of the war-torn citizenry in her native country, but when the dance is exported to another culture it seems prophetic rather than reflective.

In the United States, it is well known that trends start on the West and East coasts, and then work their way to the middle of the country. By the time a particular trend, like a clothing style, gets to the Midwest, it's passé on the coasts. A schoolgirl in New York City knows more about fashion style at this very minute than a clothing designer in Omaha, Nebraska (assuming that there are any clothing designers in Omaha, Nebraska).

Beyond that, there is the individuality of the artist to take into consideration. Some artists have a vision that surpasses their times and produce works of art that see into the

future. They are leaders. Others have a knack for discerning the pulse of a people; their genius lies in recording and playing back to us what we know intuitively to be true. They are reflectors.

Van Gogh was an artist of vision far beyond that of his culture — a leader. Norman Rockwell was skilled at depicting American life with such insight that his paintings could bring tears to the eyes of his audience — he was a reflector. And although it is the reflective type that strikes a chord with most of us, we tend to denigrate it as far as 'Art' is concerned. Rockwell is more commonly called an 'illustrator,' which is true enough but doesn't tell the whole story.

Where does this leave art in the New Age? Since art derives its meaning from the artist who conceives and produces the work, then New Age art will be found to contain elements of New Age thought in amounts equal to its influence. As we will see as this tour progresses, the production will tell on the producer and the audience as well.

Traditional artistic expressions are fading, to be sure. The ballet, symphonic orchestras, and legitimate theatre are finding that increasingly smaller segments of the population are willing to pay to see their live performances. In many countries they are heavily subsidized by the government in order to keep them alive, much as historically significant buildings have to be maintained from public funds so that they will not suffer and die from the inevitable ravages of time.

The consumer's art money is going

Dancer Wayne Sleep leads the dancers of London's Hot Shoe Show. *The success of dance shows and of musicals like* Cats *and* Evita *has continued the tradition of art as popular entertainment.*

'Concrete has never been employed more expertly, steel more frankly, but how comfortable is the place to eat and sleep and live in?'
W.G.Rodgers

into posters, popular record albums and concert performances, mass-produced furniture, best-selling paperback books, china figurines, movie viewings either at the theatre or on home video, and this year's fashion craze. No government is being asked to subsidize a Dire Straits tour (honestly, the *Guide* simply loves Dire Straits), the latest Steven Speilberg movie, or the production of miniature Eiffel Towers with digital clocks built into the base.

This has created a gap of sorts — between what we believe to be 'serious' art (better yet, Serious Art) and the sort of thing that receives our patronage.

Technology has had a tremendous impact on this gap, because 'live art' (what you get by attending a concert, visiting a museum, or commissioning the production of handcrafted furniture) is less accessible, more expensive, and demands greater participation than the art that has become so available in the wake of modern technology. So it's movies with Dolby sound, laser disc records, mass-produced posters and art prints, sculpture reproductions, weekly television shows, and designer jeans.

The art 'elitists' are (or consider themselves to be) in a different class altogether from the plebian masses who don't know a masterpiece from a conversation piece.

PEOPLE WHO LIVE IN GLASS HOUSES

Perhaps the first architectural movement to idealize the concepts of the New Age was the Bauhaus School. Founded by Walter Gropius in Weimer, Germany, in 1919, the Bauhaus School was more than a place to learn architecture — it was a commune, a spiritual movement, a philosophical center, a tank in which new artistic ideas could breed.

Buildings without decoration, walls of impersonal glass, windows that don't open . . . Such architecture has appeared all over the world, but its unpopularity has forced it into retreat.

Germany in 1919 was crushed by war, humiliated at Versailles, and literally waiting for a revolution to change everything: in other words, the obvious place to create a new world — a new age. The battle cry of Bauhaus, 'starting from zero', summarized the plan: to rise, Phoenix-like, from the post-war ashes and create something out of nothing.

Its primary goal was to fashion a non-bourgeois style. This meant architecture for the proletariat; housing for the working class. Surely, there could be no worthier goal. And toward the end of creating noble structures wherein the noble proletariat could live their noble lives, there was a studied rejection of the conventions of architecture and design that had previously signified the ruling class.

Non-bourgeois came to mean machine-made, because only the

rich could afford the hand-crafted moldings, trims, mantles and eaves of the old, passé architecture. Façades had to go (naturally), along with non-natural colors, flowerboxes hanging outside the windows, pitched roofs that suggested the crowns of the oppressors, and all luxury materials that were, financially, out of the reach of the common man.

While it may have been a well-meant gesture, there were several flaws in the Bauhaus movement. For one thing, it was managed entirely by bourgeois architects — upper-middle class men who had no idea what it was to work with their hands and struggle for their daily bread. This got the whole business off to a bad start. Additionally, in romanticizing the working class, they also robbed it of its aspirations, assuming that workers had no interest in pitched roofs, marble floors and flower boxes

outside their windows — which, of course, they did. In this way, the Bauhaus dictators practiced an artistic tyranny against those they claimed to hold most holy, believing that the noble peasant had no desire for beauty or, indeed, simple comfort.

In the late 1930s, Gropius and several of his students (most notably, Mies van der Rohe) came to the United States to escape the heat in Germany. They brought their movement with them, and the trans-Atlantic effect was so great that they pretty much overpowered everything that was going on architecturally in America at that time. The International Style was born, which is to say that the Bauhaus movement began to export its ideas internationally.

'Our concern is not how to worship in the catacombs, but how to remain human in the skyscrapers.'
Abraham Joshua Heschel

The Pompidou Center, Paris. This is a building turned inside-out, with its air ducts, water and gas pipes located on the outside.

THE SILVER SCREEN

All pilgrims know what an Art Film is, we presume? This is a movie that possesses at least three of the following attributes:

• subtitles, or dubbing
• grainy black and white or poorly exposed color film
• shown in seedy theatres; never shown in shopping-mall cinemas, or in theatres that boast more than one viewing screen
• directors and producers whose names are largely unknown to the viewing audience; or whose names are Wertmuller, Bergman, Trufaut, Fellinni
• never shown in a city of less than 3 million inhabitants
• filmed entirely on location or on a claustrophobic set designed to convey suburban angst
• very short (under one hour) or very long (over four hours)

Art films are like literary classics which, according to Mark Twain, everyone wants to have read but nobody wants to read.

Having now defined art in filmmaking (and identified films that we all would like to have seen) we can proceed to a discussion of the films we *do* see — the popular cinema.

What movies have played big in the New Age?

Citizen Kane, with its ground-breaking cinematography and brave exposé of the corruption of publishing? *On the Waterfront*, or *Rebel Without a Cause*, the battlecry for the beat generation? *Rock Around the Clock*, which brought rock 'n' roll to teenagers everywhere? *Easy Rider*, *Gandhi*, *The Graduate*, *Woodstock*, *Hair*? Maybe it's *Brave New World*, *Fahrenheit 451*, *2001*, or any of a hundred dystopic science fiction novels-turned-cinematic-achievement.

Movies are a well-mixed conglomerate of sometimes competing interests and values. On the one hand we have drama, the theatre, the soulful acting-out of human agonies and aspirations. And on the other hand, crass commercialism, the profit imperative, the mandate to create a box-office blockbuster. This marriage has created an uneasy alliance between art and mammon, and the New Age moviegoer, pandered to by profit-conscious directors, producers and actors, is chagrinned to see how his or her world outlook has been savaged by Hollywood and Pinewood.

The offerings include post-apocalypse action movies that remind us that life after the nuclear holocaust won't be pretty, even if it is barely possible; nostalgic reminiscences of what we used to believe in, movies that show us how our generation has failed itself and abandoned its dreams; films to remind us that our families are breaking down, that show us the pain of broken marriages, single parents, homosexual love and death; movies to enlighten us, to cajole us into remembering our ideals, movies that appeal to our patriotism, our humanitarianism, our brotherly love; and enigmatic blockbusters that send us out of the theatre wondering why in the world we paid good money to be terrified by the cruelty of our race.

The stereo film craze of the 1950s required viewers to wear special glasses. Audience screamed and squirmed as trains roared out of the screen, etc . . .

All over the world, large corporations and governments began to erect structures that were supported by steel beams with a thin shell of stucco, concrete and, later, glass to seal them in. The workers, and often the poor, were given big boxcar-like barracks in which to live, huge buildings with narrow hallways, a cubistic feel, and no access to green space. And then there were those big, curtainless windows that make you feel that if you aren't careful you'll topple out of your bedroom onto the pavement below.

Once considered the architecture of the New Age, they are now considered tenements. Said Saul Alinsky of such public housing in the United States: 'Originally conceived and carried through as major advances in ridding cities of slums, they involved the tearing down of rotting, rat-infested tenements, and the erection of modern apartment buildings. They were acclaimed as America's refusal to permit its people to live in the dirty shambles of the slums. It is common knowledge that they have turned into jungles of horror and now confront us with the problem of how we can either convert or get rid of them. A beautiful, positive dream has grown into a negative nightmare.'

Although the giant chrome-and-glass structures continue to be built for industrial and residential purposes, nobody confesses to believing in them anymore; what they do confess is that when the builder doesn't have to put molding around the inside doors, or make windows that actually open and close, or apply a visually appealing façade, or incorporate any number of human values into the design of the building . . . well, they're just faster and cheaper to build, that's all.

Now we are seeing the second wave in New Age architecture, and it's a movement born at the grass-roots level. It has to do with rehabbing and retrofitting old homes — buying up decaying townhouses in the heart of the city, or rescuing old farmhouses or even suburban tract homes — and endowing them with their own decorative signature. It has to do with earth-sheltered homes, solar-powered homes, and hand-built homes. The new wave concerns itself with log homes and Buckminster Fuller's geodesic dome homes. The latest in technology, in energy-aware physics, is being combined with the pervasive belief that homes are to live in, that they should be comfortable, that even if a wood-burning stove spoils 'the line' of a wall, it can be tolerated.

Industrial architecture is giving way somewhat, too. We see buildings sided with natural redwood, a return to brick facings, a departure from the flat Bauhaus roof to a pitched roof, and just the slightest hint of decorative molding on exterior and interior surfaces. But best of all, there has been a return to the idea (which never should have been abandoned) that architecture is, supremely, art for the people, and that those who will live/work/use a building should be allowed to communicate their values to the architect who will do his or her level best to create a work of art that will please the patron.

THE GALLERY SCENE

The visual art of the last century (by visual we mean drawing, painting, sculpting — that sort of thing) and all the centuries before it was very different from the art of today. Let's take the most obvious difference first: the old artists were preoccupied with the task of faithfully and accurately portraying their subject, be it a bowl of pears, a landscape, or the squire's ugly daughter (in the last case, a certain amount of subjectivity was allowed, yea, even encouraged).

The job of the artist/craftsman was to transfer actual forms of life onto

'Art, like morality, consists in drawing the line somewhere.'
G.K. Chesterton

'The artist has a special task and duty: the task of reminding men of their humanity and the promise of their creativity.'
Lewis Mumford

MUSIC, MAESTRO!

The distribution of music has always been a rather simple matter. Anybody can think up a little ditty, sing it to a friend, sing it to another friend, sing it to a group of people, and watch it go from there. No publisher needed, no expensive materials, no great investment of time, no union card.

Our musical heritage is founded on work songs, songs used for worship, songs to rally men to arms, songs recording a common history, and songs used for simple entertainment.

A rather recent function of songs, however, has been The Message. Whereas it was once enough merely to compose a tune that could be hummed by the average human voice, to find phrases that would rhyme, to convey known spiritual meaning into poetry and notes, we now expect a bit more.

The Message is the thing — in modern folk music, protest songs, songs of defiance and the ever important songs that sell us deodorant, soft drinks and laundry detergent.

Certainly we cannot say that a message was always lacking in the music of the old age, but as with the visual arts, the dynamic between truth and beauty is changing so that today's musicians would rather sacrifice beauty for truth than have it be the other way around. This is the only possible explanation for Bob Dylan singing his own songs; his voice is terrible, but the truth of what he says is so powerful that we are willing to tolerate the gravel in his throat in order to better understand the pain in his heart and the vision of his soul.

Music, like all performing arts, is obsessed with truth. This cannot be a bad thing, but it produces some bewildered audiences. Would you really enjoy a concert where two cellists play the same solitary note for forty-five minutes? Really? How about attending a dance recital in which the dancer does nothing but sit in a chair, or walk or lie on the floor for the entire performance? You're likely to end up watching a dance in a bag — literally, a dancer performing in a bag — if you're not careful. And then there is the theatre . . . But surely we're somewhat off the subject now. (Nevertheless, we were unable to find even one individual at the *Guide* who would accept the two tickets we had for 'Chairs'; it seems everyone was more interested in the Peter, Paul and Mary reunion concert than theatre of the absurd.)

Mark Knopfler, lead singer with Dire Straits.

The technology of this era has had a profound effect on the musical arts, obviously. In the old days, you couldn't possibly entertain the idea of a career as a vocalist unless you could be heard (without the benefit of electronic embellishments) in the last row of the third balcony. But today, it's enough to be able to whisper or grunt, into a microphone. Live performances were once the only means by which a musical artist could communicate with his or her audience — now, popular musicians tour only enough to keep their album sales at an acceptable level.

Technology has made music less participatory than it once was. You won't believe this, we know, but there was a time when if you wanted music you had to make it yourself. Honestly! Today, of course, if you want to have music you plug it in and let it go.

The *Guide* thanks all pilgrims for listening to this little comparative analysis of the music of yesterday and today. But where does that leave us in the New Age? In spite of Ozzy Osborne, in spite of electronics, in spite of videos and laser shows, we find that music is still called upon to transmit the values of our time. It still inspires us to action. It continues to provide a vehicle whereby we feel connected with those who, even if they aren't singing along with us, are listening along with us. And it touches our souls, it brings magic into our existence, it takes us out of our humdrum worlds and transports us into what can be.

All this is so difficult to put into words. If we could only play it for you . . .

'People compose for many reasons: to become immortal; because the pianoforte happens to be open; because they want to become a millionaire; because of the praise of friends; because they have looked into a pair of beautiful eyes; for no reason whatsoever.' Robert Schumann

'I'll play it first and tell you what it is later.' Miles Davis

Annie-Mae Bullock, better known as the singer Tina Turner.

Modern musician, John Cage. Possibly his most famous (or infamous) work was a piece called 4'3", consisting of silence 'performed' by the performer, interpreted as he or she wanted.

truth is for each individual to discover and judge, and that the transcendence of humankind is possible — through the arts, of course.

Now, truth and beauty have always been concerns of the artist, the major preoccupation of the arts. The proportions of each are changing, however. Whereas beauty was once the most important consideration (truth being allowed to suffer, as in the case of the squire's ugly daughter), it is currently truth that is experiencing a renaissance. Today's New Age artists are likely to err on the side of truth; if beauty can be found in truth, that's fine, but it's no excuse for covering up the truth. Beauty may be sacrificed.

So too may logic, or even simple consideration for one's audience. We find serious artists engaged in aesthetic dogfights, each trying to outdo the other with astoundingly bizarre artistic expressions: a paint-spattered quilt tacked up on the wall of a gallery; mangled hunks of iron I-beam welded together; dictionary definitions stenciled onto canvas (now *that's* truth for you) — definitions of the word 'nothing'; crumpled canvas propped against the wall with tree branches; rows of mud balls on grass mats; two parallel trenches dug in the desert; a coastline wrapped in rope and pink nylon; an exhibition hall piled knee deep in dirt; a gallery parking lot covered with salt; one nude woman rolling another nude woman in blue paint and then slinging her against the canvas-covered floor to the accompaniment of a chamber orchestra; guests chewing random pages torn from a book, spitting the pulp into a flask, fermenting it with yeast, distilling and bottling the mixture; the artist simply pasting his name on the gallery wall in lieu of a painting; the artist mutilating his body in the presence of horrified museum goers . . .

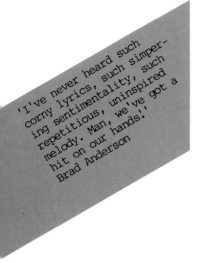

'I've never heard such corny lyrics, such simpering sentimentality, such repetitious, uninspired melody. Man, we've got a hit on our hands!'
Brad Anderson

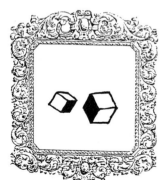

NICE... BUT IS IT ART?

THE EYE OF THE BEHOLDER

'I don't know much about art, but I know what I like,' is perhaps the most legitimate statement that can be made on the subject of aesthetics. Coming as it does from the soul of a human artist, artistic expression will be necessarily appreciated by some and misunderstood or rejected by others. This is the nature of the game; the way it is and the way it must be.

Certainly determinations may be made concerning the quality of craft exercised by the artist (one person is more skilled at laying color onto canvas, another can more accurately play the notes of a piano concerto) and a host of critics will come to a general concensus about the merits of a work of art and judge it in that way. But when we're talking about art, it is important to remember that the work gets its meaning from the creator.

Using this assumption, we may expand the term 'art' to imply everything that exists in the universe. All natural phenomena, materials and existences are the work of the first Creator, and we come to understand something of the Creator as we observe and interact with his masterpiece. We cannot say that the universe *is* the creator as animists and pantheists do; that is, that God exists in the substance of the trees, the wind, or the waters, any more than we can say that the actual soul of Rembrandt is present in or on any of his canvases. At best, we get clues to Rembrandt's soul, hints of his genius, a brief moment with him, through his work. And so it is with the Creator of the universal masterpiece.

Now, if we find the artistic expressions of our day somewhat disturbing or troublesome or unappealing, then we would do well to admit to ourselves that our entire age is disturbing, troubling and unappealing. The artists — whether we believe that they are leading us or merely playing back what we are to ourselves — are telling us about our times. We should listen.

Art is the tangible expression of an individual's most dearly held beliefs, values and personal treasures. If we feel cheated by a book, mocked by a gallery showing, or exploited by a building, then we may look to the creator of the artistic expression for an explanation.

Wouldn't it have been wonderful if the noble proletariat of Germany that was consigned to live in the Bauhaus cubes had called the elitist architects into some kind of accountability for their designs? Challenged their assumptions? 'Look here, you, I may work with my hands, and I may be downtrodden, but you've got me all wrong if you think I like living in these stark, steel-and-cement cubes whose colors nauseate me, and make me feel incarcerated. How very bourgeois of you to assume that I don't like overstuffed chairs, slanted roofs that repel the snow and rains,

and flowerboxes outside my windows.'

Certainly, the artist must answer for his work — it's only right. Claus Oldenburg must tell us all, now, why he saw fit to grace the city of Chicago with an oversized steel rendering of a baseball bat; Stephen King may be called upon to explain exactly why it is that he wants to scare the life out of us; AC-DC might be reasonably asked to elaborate on their quasi musical expression.

Of course, this is not very popular. We view artists as geniuses (whether they are or not), prophets (ditto), and sometimes, rarely, gods.

A British block of flats, built in the 1960s, is demolished in the 1980s. Many such housing projects — originally seen in Utopian terms — have ended up as slums or as piles of rubble.

Marilyn Diptych *by Andy Warhol, 1962. Warhol's work commented on the repetitious nature of mass culture — whether it was through advertising and packaged products, or about celebrities and their clones.*

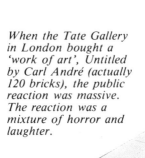

'I wonder whether what we are publishing now is worth cutting down trees to make paper for the stuff.'
Richard Brautigan

canvas or into sculpture. All that began to change in the 19th century. Although there were concurrent causes, the *Guide* is partial to the theory that the change came about largely due to the fact that with the photographic camera, images could be accurately and perfectly recorded on film. It was therefore no longer required of the artist to accomplish this task. Artists were free to move into other areas.

However it was, art began to take on a distinctly subjective quality. The strokes on the canvas, or the mass of the sculpture was used, as never

before, to convey the personality and vision of the artist. This coincided with the demise of craft, craft being the skill possessed by an artist and used successfully to transmit the reality of life to the reality of canvas or clay. Craft was once the very backbone of art, but when subjectivity invaded the visual arts, then craft began to suffer. Technology contributed to its demise as well, and the present state of affairs is that the visual arts are viewed almost entirely as a personal expression of the artist. The artist, confident that his or her personal vision is sufficient unto the task, may adopt a take-it-or-leave-it attitude toward craft, deeming it unimportant. Since art is subjective, so is technique, and one's ability to apply paint skillfully is less important than the reason that the paint is being applied in the first place. Indeed, many artists today are involved in only the conceptual work of their productions, hiring out the execution of their ideas to students and underlings.

Modern Art, with its emphasis on subjectivity and disregard for craft, is very New Age in that it promotes the idea that the individual is supreme,

When the Tate Gallery in London bought a 'work of art', Untitled by Carl André (actually 120 bricks), the public reaction was massive. The reaction was a mixture of horror and laughter.

THE MAKING OF MANY BOOKS

Literature, perhaps more than any other kind of artistic expression, has faithfully chronicled the New Age. A host of fiction and non-fiction works, many already ascribed 'classic' status, present the gospel of the 20th century to anyone who can read — or knows someone who can.

The papers of Sigmund Freud, the ravings of Jack Kerouac, the Saul Alinsky rulebooks, the poems of Timothy Leary, the dire predictions of Rachel Carson, the cynicism of Ayn Rand and Bertrand Russell, Darwin's theories, Kurt Vonnegut's satirical science fiction, Margaret Mead's anthropological observations, Kubler-Ross's research on death and dying, a host of pop psychology how-to-help-yourself-help-yourself books, and thousands of other provocative volumes — all this might have died on the vine in another century, or been disseminated only to the intelligensia, or communicated only to those with similar, esoteric concerns. But in this generation — with its high degree of literacy and its prolific publishing industry — the thinking of the world's great philosophers, teachers and crack-pots has been disseminated to the mainstream of the population.

Once confined to ivory towers, these ideas and observations are now readily available at train-station news stands, in chain bookstores, and through the mail.

Tremendous opportunity . . . or unbelievable danger? Who knows? Some say that while the scholars are trying desperately to make their research and ideas palatable for the masses, determined to publish or perish, and while opportunists with half-baked ideas are searching for the respectability that publishing brings, the unsuspecting public is being fed a mixed diet of great wisdom side-by-side with great folly, and they simply don't know the difference between the two.

The truth, or at least serious attempts at it, gets the same packaging as tripe. A hardback book by Hans Küng looks, feels and costs pretty much the same as a hardback book by Van Daniken . . . and there are those who will read both and develop their opinions not so much on the merit of the argument as on the lucidity of the author's writing style, the presence of helpful illustrations and diagrams, and the wit and humor of the author's editor.

Egalitarian New Agers don't hold with such elitist snobbery, though. 'Let the people decide,' say they. 'We don't need any dictators, detractors or censors to tell *us* how to think. We can figure it out for ourselves. And who are you to say that one is true and the other false? Remember what age you're in, buddy, before you start pushing a bunch of absolutes down our throats.'

In addition to exposure to the best (and worst — we regrettably say) thinkers of our time, we are also getting to read the philosophers and thinkers of past ages. Certainly the thought of Plato, Socrates, Christ and Augustine is more widely-known today than it was in their own day.

Danger or opportunity? Opinions vary. That the look, feel and inherent respectability of publishing can disguise the lack of substance in a particular tome; or that the 'masses' are often poorly equipped to distinguish between a serious book worthy of serious consideration and a catchy idea poshed up to look like something more than it is, is arguably dangerous.

But the *Guide* will side with those who say that the opportunity is more important than the danger is threatening.

'A bad book is as much a labor to write as a good one, it comes as sincerely from the author's soul.' Aldous Huxley

'A book is the only place in which you can examine a fragile thought without breaking it, or explore an explosive idea without fear it will go off in your face . . . it is one of the few havens remaining where a man's mind can get both provocation and privacy.' Edward P. Morgan

'These are not books, lumps of lifeless paper, but *minds* alive on the shelves. From each of them goes out its own voice . . . and just as the touch of a button on our set will fill the room with music, so by taking down one of these volumes and opening it, one can call into range the voice of a man·far distant in time and space, and hear him speaking to us, mind to mind, heart to heart.' Gilbert Highet

'This novel is not to be tossed lightly aside, but to be hurled with great force.' Dorothy Parker

'That's not writing, that's typing!' Truman Capote, of Jack Kerouac

Consequently, we have embarrassed ourselves by lapping up whatever they put in the dish. It is the opinion of the *Guide* that this genuflection before the altar of art must cease.

For calling artists into accountability is far preferable to calling art to answer for itself. In the words of Hans Rookmaaker, art needs no justification. It is what it is. It is expression, and as such, needs no other purpose than to be — like tears, laughter, and kisses. It is enough that they exist.

This is not to say that what we call art is always without guile. Just as a kiss may betray, or tears may manipulate, or laughter can ring false, art too may be used for false purposes. It may be used to manipulate an audience, or exploit its patrons. But, luckily, every now and then someone unafraid to speak his mind will get up and declare to the world, 'The Emperor has no clothes . . .' May we all be so brave and self-assured!

> 'You cannot paint or sing yourselves into being good men; you must be good men before you can either sing or paint, and then color and sound will complete in you all that is best.'
> John Ruskin

FAITH AND THE ARTS

Christians affirm the idea that we are living in the midst of a masterpiece of art (the universe) and that we are encouraged to be good caretakers of that work of art. Similarly, they recognize the value of creating artistic works of beauty and truth themselves.

The arts are used to describe the indescribable, define the indefinable, express the inexpressible, and explain the unknowable. The arts are appreciated for their ability to shortcut the intellect and the conventions of culture to define the aesthetic reality of human nature.

The expression may be obviously 'Christian' — as in Michelangelo's 'David,' da Vinci's 'The Last Supper,' or Hook's 'Jesus,' Or it may be completely lacking in overt religious symbolism, as are the works of many popular musicians, authors, designers and sculptors who profess faith in Jesus Christ. But no matter. It's art. One expression is not necessarily superior to another, although different artists may believe that they have a call to work in one medium or another.

The important thing is that since any work of art is a message from the soul of the artist to his own Creator and his own contemporaries, Christian artists cannot help but produce works of art that express the beauty, truth and goodness of God. Art needs no justification.

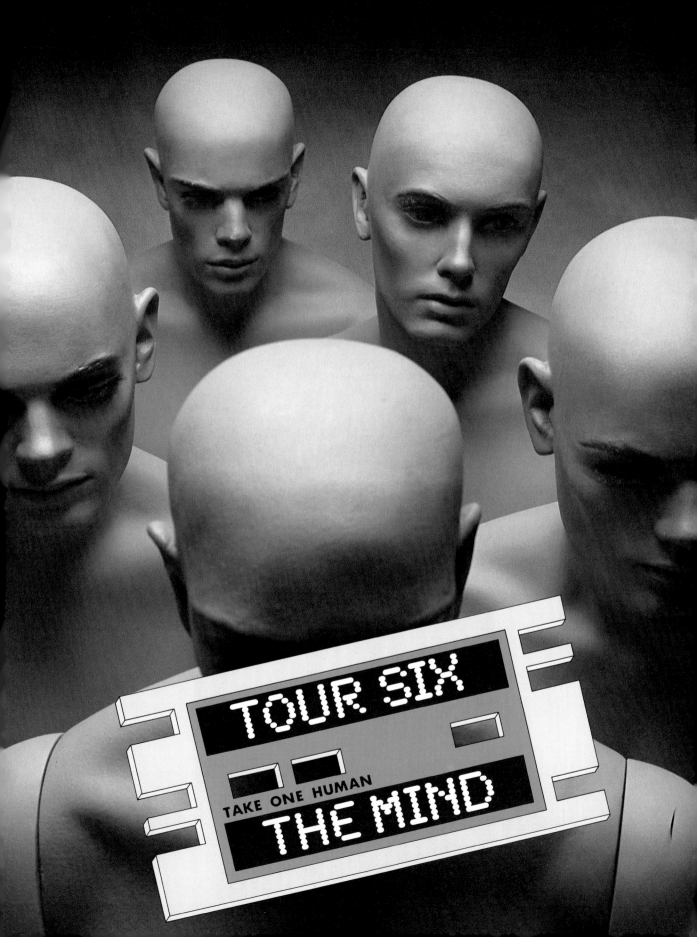

CONSCIOUSNESS

Metaphors seem the only adequate language with which to discuss consciousness. Why is this? Perhaps it is that we need consciousness to discuss consciousness. Maybe our minds just like to show off what they know, constructing elaborate 'It's just like . . .' statements with which to impress ourselves and others. Conscious minds make corrections; they sort and tag things for future reference.

Unfortunately, it is also much easier to figure out what consciousness *isn't* than what it *is*. For example:

● **Consciousness doesn't have anything to do with getting 'knocked out'** as in, 'he lost consciousness.'

● **Consciousness is not merely a perception,** as when someone says, 'I wasn't conscious of the fact' (invariably when they're stepping on your foot on a crowded bus).

● **Consciousness is not necessary for day-to-day living.** As a matter of fact, the average pilgrim's day is full of activities that are performed in the absence of full consciousness: reaching for a doorknob, blinking your eyes, riding a bicycle or running down the street. All of these, if done consciously, would be extremely difficult to execute. If you doubt it, try climbing a flight of stairs, paying attention to every motion of your feet, legs, arms, torso and head. Even breathing becomes difficult under such circumstances!

● **Consciousness probably does not occupy any square footage in the brain.** That is, there is no known location of consciousness, as there is for speech or memory or growth.

Defining consciousness is a little like defining self: you can try to do it, but it's better if you just *know* what it is. But since we're getting paid for our expertise, the *Guide* will, at this time, attempt a definition: *Consciousness exists when one becomes conscious of it.*

Oh? That doesn't help? Then listen to this litle story: A man, having looted a city, was trying to sell an exquisite rug, one of the spoils. 'Who will give me 100 pieces of gold for this rug?' he cried throughout the town.

After the sale was completed, a comrade approached the seller, and asked, 'Why did you not ask more for that priceless rug?'

'Is there any number higher than 100?' asked the seller.

Did you enjoy that story? You are probably conscious. Did it escape you? You're probably not all that conscious.

Since most people these days are conscious at least part of the time (especially any person who would be interested in taking such an arduous journey through the New Age) we will proceed on the assumption that you got the joke.

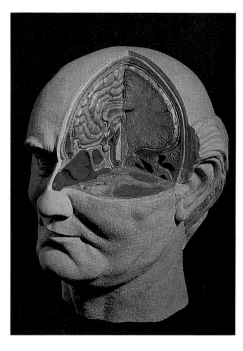

The human brain has been described as 'the only lump of matter we know from the inside'. In structure the brain is more complicated than a star, and it is an area of inner space that is constantly being explored.

TWO MINDS ARE BETTER THAN ONE

The Origin of Consciousness in the Breakdown of the Bicameral Mind, a book by Julian Jaynes, hypothesizes that in ages past, humans were in possession of a mind with two separate chambers (thus, bicameral — just as a pair of binoculars has two lenses) neither of which possessed consciousness. One of the chambers, says Jaynes, was executive in nature — call it god. The other was a follower; it acted on orders from god — call it man.

Ancient myth is full of recorded instances where people would hear the god chamber tell them what to do when confronted with a novel situation. The *Illiad*, for example, contains many passages where a god tells someone to carry out very specific instructions. Most experts in ancient literature have merely chalked such things up to the fact that the *Illiad* is pure myth, a fiction, or at least a fictionalized account of actual events. But Jaynes postulates that Achilles and all the other characters really did hear a god tell them to do this or go there, because they were in possession of a bicameral mind. They 'heard' voices.

Compare the *Illiad* with the *Odyssey*. While some scholars believe that both were written by Homer, that's doubtful. The *Odyssey* was probably written a hundred or so years later. And in the *Odyssey* we see, according to Jaynes, an instance of the breakdown of the bicameral mind and the origins of consciousness. The gods, now, are all but silent. They don't speak as they once did. The sense of good and evil, completely absent in the *Illiad*, are very much present in the *Odyssey*, as are deceit and guilt — definite signs of consciousness.

There are not many people around today who hear voices (or admit to

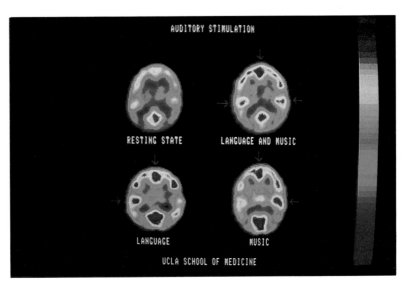

AUDITORY STIMULATION

RESTING STATE   LANGUAGE AND MUSIC

LANGUAGE   MUSIC

UCLA SCHOOL OF MEDICINE

This brain scan shows the effect upon regions of the brain of different types of sound.

it), but a few do. They're called schizophrenics. People suffering from what we call 'split personalities' often hear voices telling them what to do, but they're not the only ones. People who generally enjoy perfect mental health also hear voices from time to time, especially during times of extreme stress — either physical, emotional, or psychological. The sensation of 'hearing' voices can also be produced in the laboratory by electrically stimulating the right cerebral lobe of the brain. So there you go.

Well, Jaynes's theories are absolutely fascinating. They encompass everything from schizophrenia to poetry to art to ancient idols to hypnotic theory. And if it all sounds pretty noo-noo-na-na to you, then let's look into some facts about the physiology of the brain that are very well documented by some very conservative physiologists.

LEFT, RIGHT, LEFT, RIGHT . . .

'I'm left-brained; I have to read it before I believe it.'

'I'm right-brained; that's why I sit

Exploring the inner space of the mind can be hazardous. Some thinkers see the rational mind as an obstacle to reality. The truth can only be discovered by bypassing the rational mind through drugs and hallucinations. The majority of thinkers on the subject, however, only trust the mind when it is undisturbed and healthy.

in front of television all day.'

Are you kidding? 'Left-brained?' 'Right-brained?'

Important parts of the human body are typically dispensed by nature in sets of two: two eyes, two kidneys, two lungs, two arms, two legs. Nature is generous; she recognizes the possibility that one organ or limb will be damaged, and provides an extra just in case.

The brain is no exception; it consists of two hemispheres, right and left. In some ways they are duplicates of one another. But they also have unique functions, which is obvious to anyone who has worked with stroke patients. In nearly every case, a stroke that paralyzes the right side of the body causes loss of speech for the patient. Not always, but nearly so. That's because speech is located on the left side of the brain.

Did you get that? The left side of the brain stores motor skills for the right side of the body. So damage to the left side of the brain often paralyzes the right side of the body.

Although human beings are born with brains that weigh the same on the left as they do on the right, socialization (it is thought) causes one or the other side to become slightly more developed, and that increases its weight. So if you would put your own brain hemispheres on a scale and compare them, you'd know which side is the most developed. There's an easier way. For one thing, most right-handed people have a dominant

left-brain; most left-handed people have a dominant right-brain; most ambidextrous people have ambidextrous brains.

Obviously, being left-brained is a very Western characteristic. As the Left-brain, Right-brain chart shows, left-brained people tend to be logical, linear in their thinking and verbally oriented. That's the West for you.

Right-brainers, on the other hand, are more non-rational, prone to follow their hunches, visions, and dreams. They are intuitive, passionate and creative. Meet the East.

This newly-popularized knowledge about right- and left-brain domination has affected many areas of our lives. We realize that some people need pictures to learn, while some need words. Traffic signs that used to just *tell* us what not to do now *show* us as well.

Advertisements on American television now have captions to go along with the picture, so that no segment of the market will fail to understand the pitch. Schools, which have in the past taught the left-brained (presenting virtually all their information to students via the printed word, lectures, and in a logical, linear fashion), have expanded their audio-visual resources to accommodate students who learn better by seeing and doing. And this *Guide* is loaded with pictures so that if you're less inclined to read than to look, you can still enjoy the trip.

Left-Brain Characteristics	Right-Brain Characteristics
controls speech	controls movement
right-sided motor skills (right handedness)	left-sided motor skills (left-handedness)
stores information logically, linearly, rationally	relies on hunches, visions, dreams, and non-rational thoughts
'masculine'	'feminine'
concerned with time	concerned with space
logical	intuitive
seat of reason	seat of passion
dominant with writers, mathematicians and scientists	dominant with artists, crafts-people and musicians
'verbal people'	'picturing people'
craves words	craves images

INTELLIGENCE

Intelligence: what IQ tests measure.

Now, there's a dead-end definition for you. No, there's got to be a better way to define intelligence. Let's try again.

Intelligence: the ability to perceive logical relationships and use one's knowledge to solve problems and respond appropriately to novel situations.

Certainly that's much better. Already, though, we're wondering if there's any intelligence test that can measure what is covered in that definition. How about this:

Intelligence: linguistic, logical-mathematical, musical, spatial, bodily-kinesthetic, inter-personal, and intra-personal competencies.

That's a likeable definition, since it's obvious that any reasonably normal person is likely to be competent (or even to excell) in one or more of those areas. We wouldn't call a world-class boxer stupid simply because he can't add 2 + 2. Under this definition, his bodily-kinesthetic abilities could serve as the basis for

ascertaining his intelligence. Adding all areas of human expression to the definition does tend to bring people like Einstein down a notch (we don't think he was very musical) and the presence of that element of interpersonal relationships in the

Different brains develop different physical or mental skills. While Einstein could not 'dance like a butterfly, sting like a bee' (as Mohammad Ali), he was good at physics.

THE SAVANT SYNDROME

Leslie Lemke has an IQ of about thirty, is completely blind, and crippled by cerebral palsy. He spoke his first few halting words at the age of twenty-six. He can walk now, at the age of thirty-four, only by holding on to furniture or a fence. Yet his hands move with incredible dexterity across the keyboard of his piano, duplicating any and every composition he has ever heard, in the style of the pianist who performed it from Daniel Barenboim to Elton John. He likes to sing, as he plays during his concerts, 'My Way,' 'I Believe,' 'Amazing Grace' and 'He Touched Me.'

Richard Wawro is legally blind, diabetic, and mentally retarded. He spoke his first intelligible word at the age of eleven. His oil crayon drawings, skillfully composed and rendered, depict with great sensitivity scenes viewed only fleetingly. They hang in the galleries of his native Edinburgh, as well as across Europe and North America.

Alonzo Clemons, also mentally retarded, can faithfully reproduce in sculptured wax any animal that he has seen once — whether on the hoof or from photographs. He lives in

Colorado, busy at the task of casting his works into bronze.

Once called idiot savants ('learned idiots') — now called simply savants — the gifted retarded have psychologists, psychiatrists, medical doctors and everyone they meet amazed and delighted. How is it that these severely handicapped individuals, many of them autistic, can produce such outstanding work and operate on a level far superior to many of the more talented 'normal' people?

One theory is that severe

damage or arrested development in the left-brain has resulted in an extraordinary development of the right-brain where, as you remember, are located the centers for spacial understanding, intuitive thinking, and the inclinations required for artistic performance of all kinds. The savants appear to have at least one ability that the general population lacks: they can concentrate totally on what they are doing, completely shutting out the distractions that prevent others from devoting themselves 100 per cent to the task at hand.

stew means that the hostess-with-the-mostest may claim superior intelligence on the basis of her social abilities, even if she can't discuss high-energy physics 'intelligently' with her guests.

Even in that broad definition, though, is an understanding that an intelligent person knows how to solve problems, be it how to knock his opponent out before the ninth round, how to relate energy to matter, or how to draw a shy guest out of himself so he can enjoy a dinner party.

If that seems ambiguous, who cares?

Since the eminent French psychologist Alfred Binet began looking for ways to measure the memory, imagery, attention, comprehension, judgment, and other mental functions of young children in 1894, who *doesn't* care?

Binet's idea was that each child was born with a certain amount of mental potential, and that if the degree of potential could be detected early in life, the child (more specifically, the child's parents, teachers and future employers) would be able realistically to chart a course of education and training suitable to the child's innate skills.

+

=

?

A child who scored high would be encouraged (forced?) to pursue a professional career for which he or she would receive rigorous academic preparation. High-scoring children could expect distinguished careers in the law, or medicine.

A child who scored poorly would be consigned to a menial occupation — factory work perhaps, or failing that politics — at an early stage, thereby saving everybody a lot of time, effort, and money that might otherwise be wasted trying to improve the unimproveable.

But wait, there's more. As intelligence tests continued to be used, and a larger population was subjected to their evaluation, it was noted that

some children, as a group, did more poorly than others — most notably children whose shade of skin ran to the darker hues.

Well, this invaluable news came at a time when some people were especially interested in stemming the tide of darker persons, and eugenicists were all agog over the possibility of identifying superior and inferior people, so that they could breed individuals with desirable attributes and kill, sterilize, or otherwise weed out those with undesirable traits — you know, epileptics, the feebleminded, and youngsters who carry blaring radios the size of small steamer trunks in public places.

The really appalling thing about all this, something that was accepted by virtually the entire academic community, was that intelligence was assumed to be fixed at conception. It was totally unaffected by your experience after that point (so don't give us any of your liberal bleeding heart nonsense about non-existent educational opportunities for blacks, latinos, etc . . .). Even when evidence was presented to the contrary by some brave researchers — showing that remedial programs for those with holes in their education and experience could raise intelligence scores — the establishment insisted that their tests were invalid.

It's less popular these days to believe that lower test scores in any social groups should be attributed to radical differences in racial intelligence, but the belief has not been totally extinguished. You've heard, or course, about the sperm bank whose depositors are Nobel Prize winners, and from which those women who wish to make withdrawals must meet certain criteria in terms of beauty, 'intelligence,' creativity, and so on.

Until we get a firmer understanding of what intelligence is (one that everyone can agree on) it's going to be hard to carry out valid measurements of mental skill at all. And, of course, there will always be a few boat-rockers who believe that the notion of measuring such things is flawed in its very soul, and that firm understanding or no, it should not be done.

TO SLEEP, TO DREAM

The ancient peoples had no problem at all dealing with their dreams. They believed that dreams were omens from the gods, portents of events to come, manifestations of higher powers. Scientific Age thinkers rejected such notions almost completely. Some of them even said that dreams just didn't exist.

It is possible that they came to this conclusion because they had never had a dream that they could *remember*. This is common. We remember only the smallest fraction of our dreams in the first place, and many people don't remember any dreams at all. These folks take some convincing on the point that yes, you do dream, every night, like everyone else.

Research into the mechanics of sleep have shown that there are different stages of sleep — we move through the stages all night long. One stage, characterized by rapid eye movements on the part of the sleeper (REM sleep), is the one where dreaming is most likely to occur. This is a deep sleep stage and not the one in which most people waken

A modern verdict on sleep and dreams: 'Sleep is when all the unsorted stuff comes flying out as from a dustbin upset in a high wind.' William Golding

naturally, so by the time they have emerged from REM sleep, the dream is far behind them. Since dreams tend to be fairly elusive to begin with, the sleeper often wakens with no memory of the dream. But just try waking them up during the REM stage (which is easy to detect since their eyeballs are revolving all over the place) and they can tell you *exactly* what they've dreamed. Even then, by morning it's likely that they won't remember the dream, nor what they said in the middle of the night.

Everybody dreams. Interestingly, if dreams are for some reason prevented during normal sleep, they will happen spontaneously during the day. First there will be daydreams, and if interruption continues there will be full-blown hallucinations. Serious problems arise if dream interruption persists. Immanuel Kant, who once said, 'The madman is a waking dreamer', had no way of knowing how absolutely factual his statement was.

It was Freud who, in the midst of Victorian scientism, reintroduced the concept that dreams are important, that they have something to say, and the individual who listens to his dreams can learn something — usually about himself. He called dreams the Royal Road to the Unconscious. He did a lot of dream analysis, and in the course of his work arrived at a number of common symbols present in dreams, and their supposed interpretation. For Freud, all dreams were significant. (As far as we know, Freud never blamed especially bizarre dreams on extra anchovies and pineapple on the midnight pizza.) In Freud's lexicon, dreaming about an Emperor or Empress (or a King, Queen, President or what have you) signifies one's parents; rooms are women; entrances and exits are the body; sharp weapons, tree trunks

DREAM SYMBOLISM

When you dream about this . . .	It is said to symbolize . . .
house	self
attic	conscious mind
tower	superconscious (it towers over all)
cellar	subconscious
hallway	transition or change
scales	justice
scissors	death or separation
gun	emotional explosions
bathroom	cleansing needed
fireplace	comfort, purification, digestion
eraser	eliminating faults
oil	removing friction
yeast	increasing
arrow	message coming
sliding downhill	danger
flying	wishful thinking
dwarf	inadequacy
gardener	attainment of beauty
elevator	depression/optimism
fire	lust, blazing anger
crowd	hidden guilt
eating	love
passenger	passivity
missing a train	failure
police	authority, protection, punishment of conscience
running	goal achievement

and sticks are male genitalia while cupboards, boxes, and ovens are female (at this point I think we know quite a bit about Freud, if not ourselves!).

In the quest for expanded consciousness in the New Age, dreams are receiving ever more attention. Prophetic dreams (those that predict the future, such as the death of a loved one or some other epochal personal event) are given credence, as well as those that seem to be trying to unlock a hitherto closed door of consciousness. The idea that dreams are instructive about the self is highly attractive as far as most of us are concerned, hence the rise in the popularity of keeping dream journals.

PSYCHO-PATHOLOGY

If the range of possible human behavior exists on a scale, it has always been a prickly task for society to figure out what to do with the people whose thoughts and actions are on the extreme edges of the scale — or even off it. These are the people whose lives are characterized by confusion, disorientation, profound apathy, hallucinations, hyperactivity, acute excitement, catatonia, astonishingly optimistic or depressive states.

Often called 'mad' or 'insane', people like these who pushed the limits of acceptability used to be excluded from the mainstream of society, ridiculed, abused, imprisoned, and sometimes killed outright. Ancient cultures were likely to attribute their actions to demonic possession, and given that diagnosis the penalties were often severe.

We now believe that behavior is a combination of one's genetic inheritance, physical and social environments, and personal life experiences. We reject the 'disease' model as an explanation for deviant behavior; we have great sympathy for those who are so different. We sense that on the human behavior scale, they are just a little bit nearer to the edge of the scale than most of us, and that with the proper help these unfortunates can be pulled back towards the middle.

Indeed, there is sometimes a romanticizing of what used to be considered pathological behavior. Many of us actually seek abnormality, in a sense, taking drugs in hopes of having consciousness-raising hallucinations, drinking coffee so that we will be more alert, drinking to forget, taking sedatives to cure excitement, and deliberately concentrating on competing thoughts in the hope of producing mental disorientation.

It was popular, during the Scientific Age, to attribute all 'abnormal' behavior to one's *nature*; that is, inherited characteristics, 'bad blood', organic imbalances or other kinds of disease (in exactly the same way that intelligence was thought completely innate). In the New Age, we blame *nurture*, or one's environment and experiences since birth. As with Maslow's hierarchy of needs (see Tour Two: The Self), which assumes that

Modern mentally ill patients at an art therapy class.

our environment prevents us from actualizing ourselves, it is believed that pathological environmental conditions cause some people to take on aberrant behavior and to indulge in confused thought processes.

Even though schizophrenia is now being found to be responsive to megavitamin therapy (and also to run in families) and psychosurgery is coming into its own as a fully legitimate practice, we still blame *first* society, an individual's family life, and other external influences for his or her abnormal behavior.

PSI

Psi, originally short for para-psychology, consists of a number of phenomena that cannot easily be explained by traditional scientific definitions. It covers:

● **Telepathy:** the communication from one person to another through some means other than the senses — mind-reading and the like.

● **Clairvoyance:** discerning objects not present to the senses (broadly referred to as ESP — Extra Sensory Perception) in such activities as describing a shape on a hidden card.

● **Precognition:** telepathy or clairvoyance relating to future events or situations; future-sight of any kind.

● **Psychokenesis:** influencing physical objects by willing a particular outcome (like Uri Geller and his bending spoons).

To those who believe in psi power, no scientific proof or empirical evidence is needed; for those who disbelieve, none is adequate. Where parapsychology is concerned, most of us tend to fall on one side of the fence or the other. Of course, we have our lapses: the person with a supernaturalist bent occasionally falls into fits of doubt, and the naturalist may find himself caught up in a flight of fancy, admitting that the idea of The Great Beyond is mightily persuasive.

And if demonstrations of Extra Sensory Perception were confined to spoon-bending in night clubs, mock-seances at school girls' slumber parties, or the occasional 'I saw that Charlie was going to lose the Irish Sweepstakes' from the lips of Great-Aunt Agatha, the *Guide* would make this a short stop indeed.

But of course the subject goes well beyond such benign claims and experiences. Respected educational institutions around the world now offer classes and even graduate degrees in parapsychology. Research labs — private and public — are receiving heavy funding from government and private foundations. Sick people are flying to the Philippines to undergo psychic surgery for a variety of illnesses. Advanced Transcendental Meditators are instructed on how to levitate. Major building projects are determined by a divining rod. A city in New York State recently retained the services of an aura-reader who sits at the right hand of the Public Defender, offering psychic judgments about the suitability of prospective jurors.

Then there is the everyday fallout:

ROSE-TINTED GLASSES

In *The Road Less Traveled*, psychiatrist M. Scott Peck hypothesizes, on the basis of his extensive clinical work, that neuroses, personality disorders, and even some psychoses are the result of lack of discipline in the individual who suffers from the illness. For some reason — by virtue of inability or unwillingness, either of which may be the result of unfortunate early childhood experiences — they refuse to face up to the hard facts of life.

His patients, he found, cherished unrealistic expectations about life, usually along the order of believing that life should be easy, everything rosy, and other people co-operative when in fact the exact opposite is more often true.

Rather than confront such painful realities, these unrealistic and indisciplined individuals resort to neurotic or psychotic behavior — as though they'd rather be proven crazy than wrong.

millions of people planning their lives around the predictions of palmreaders and spiritualists, countless thousands living in hopes of communicating with dead loved ones, and incredible sums of money spent and collected by practitioners of the psychic arts.

When otherwise normal people succumb in numbers to the seduction of the paranormal, what help can be offered the unsuspecting pilgrim as he or she journeys through the unknown? As we have already stated, naturalists and supernaturalists disagree.

'But look,' the intrepid parapsychologist points out, 'Psi, by its very nature being supernatural and extra-sensory, certainly defies any kind of scientific or empirical verification. The fact that psi phenomena cannot be ''proven'' scientifically agrees with the fact that they exist in a separate sphere of reality. Just because a particular effect *may* be reproduced by trickery does not prove a thing.'

Of course, this is true, and as long as the discussion and all activities take place on that 'extra-reality' plane, no one can really disagree. That is why religious beliefs (which do not lay claim to any scientific proof for their assertions) generally remain exempt from any talk of proofs. But occasionally, the extra-sensory (like the religious) impinges on the sensory (or the secular), as when confessed supernaturalists venture to show physical proof for their beliefs. At this point, they invite inquiry.

Put another way, as long as the discussion is kept strictly in terms of the supernatural, it should be allowed to stay there. If, for example, a husband and wife argue that they are able, through a 'sixth-sense', to anticipate each other's thoughts and actions, and verify the fact with an explanation on the order of: 'Well, we just know — that's how', they may be excused from further scrutiny.

But if they offer *proof* in physical terms, like: 'Fred comes home from

work at a different time every night, and nine out of ten times I am able to predict — at 12:00 noon — what time he will walk in the door, within two minutes'; and should Mr and Mrs Fred start offering classes on their brand of telepathy, sell tapes on how to develop the technique, or go on the talk-show circuit with their act — then they are inviting scientific investigation.

The *Guide* maintains that when psi believers become psi practitioners; when they make specific claims to the public; when they charge for their services; when they offer medical care for the ill; when they derive personal benefit or attention from their alleged abilities to perform, then they should be investigated scientifically.

What's the fuss? It's just for fun, you may say. And so have others. In

Uri Geller, an Israeli psychic, became famous in the early 1970s for his ability to bend spoons and stop watches by the power of thought. These frames from a film show how Geller snapped a spoon apparently by simply rolling his thumb and index finger over it.

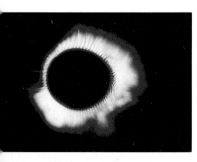

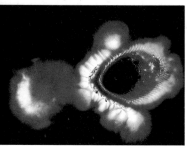

Kirlian photography (discovered by Soviet doctor Semyon Kirlian in 1939) is said to reveal the electrical current surrounding living organisms. These two Kirlian photographs show Uri Geller's fingertip at rest, and during 'a burst of energy'.

closing on this very serious subject we quote from James Randi ('The Amazing Randi'), a magician by trade, who has made quite a study of parapsychological phenomena. His prowess in sleight-of-hand, illusion, distraction and other skills of the professional magician have uniquely qualified him to investigate the claims of many who may be employing similar techniques and passing them off to the scientific community as true psychic ability. Says Randi:

'Many "men of science" stupidly assume that because they have been trained in the physical sciences or the medical arts, they are capable of flawless judgment in the investigation of alleged psychics. Nothing could be further from the truth. In fact, the more scientifically trained a person's mind, the more he or she is apt to be duped by an enterprising performer. A scientist's test tube will not lie; another human being will. Scientists are all the more easily deceived because they think in a logical manner.'

HYPNOSIS

'You are sitting in this chair, and you are listening to my voice and your eyelids are getting heavy, and they are beginning to close . . .'

Thus begins the professional hypnotist who is going to explore areas of the mind unavailable to the normally awake, normally conscious person.

There are many theories that describe how or why hypnosis works (or can't work) and what it may or may not be good for. Most experts in the field agree that it is an enhancement of the individual's innate suggestibility. Thus, some people are more prone to suggestibility than others: they are much more likely to carry out a suggested act without processing the suggestion logically. For example, if asked 'Don't you feel thirsty?' the

highly suggestible person will reach for a drink without considering whether or not he or she is indeed thirsty.

At some point, suggestibility becomes hypnotism — no one knows exactly where. A real estate agent may say to a customer, 'Yes, that house is truly lovely, but I don't know if I should let you see the inside of it or not, because it's priced a bit higher than you can afford, and *just looking at it will make you want to buy it.*' Said in the right tone of voice, with good eye contact, with the proper degree of trust established between agent and potential buyer, that sentence could indeed be considered more than merely a suggestion, but a *hypnotic* suggestion.

So what is hypnosis? The literal meaning of the word lies with Hypnos, the Greek god of sleep (the Romans called the same guy Somnus — get the connection?). Some people say it's a sleep-like state that is specially induced; others contend that it is quite the opposite — a relaxed state in which the senses are heightened, a superalert state in which the subject is able to think more clearly and effectively.

How ever it is, the hypnotic state may be induced by outside help (usually a medical doctor, psychologist, or other practitioner) or by yourself: self-hypnosis. Popularly, hypnosis is associated with nightclub performers who use the method to further the science of entertainment, by suggesting that selected volunteers strut like chickens, imitate their most admired person, or hold an arm perpendicular to the body for an extended period of time. All good fun.

More serious applications have been in the area of psychoanalysis, where patients are placed in a hypnotic state in order to recall events in their childhood that may be causing present-day neuroses and psychoses; in criminal courts, where victims may recall details of a crime under hypnosis, in the hope of convicting perpetrators; in education, where students are hypnotized in order to decrease test anxiety, increase recall, and inspire brilliance; in the treatment of such diverse medical conditions as obesity, baldness, bed-wetting, acne, hair loss and high blood pressure.

The truthfulness of the many enthusiastic claims on the part of practitioners has yet to be proven in most cases. The practical application of hypnosis is still in infant stages.

Although few who have studied the phenomenon reject its validity completely, many of the best experts are most cautious about its virtues. In the case of using a crime victim's hypnotic recollections as testimony, some experts maintain that the very suggestibility inherent in hypnosis is likely to combine the subject's fantasies, unrelated memories of other events, and communications from the hypnotist, and fuse this jumbled assemblage into a story that will pass for fact. This then creates problems for innocent associates, acquaintances, or chance bystanders who might have a place in the victim's consciousness, but who could be incorrectly associated with the crime.

Some psychiatrists maintain that hypnotic memory is, in most cases, actually less accurate than normal, waking recall; it has been demonstrated that hypnotized subjects try to please investigators by providing the answers they think the questioner wants to hear. That's obviously a poor place to start when trying to figure out The Whole Truth and Nothing But the Truth.

THE SPIRITUAL MIND

Earlier, the *Guide* stated that Christian thought holds in high esteem the cosmos, the self, the family, the body, the arts, and

reformation. Now (and it should come as no surprise) we will propose that the mind, too, has a place of importance in Christian thinking.

Freud distinguished between the conscious, unconscious and subconscious mind; psychologists often talk of mental health versus mental illness, indicating a split between a well mind and a sick mind. For scientists there is the rational mind as opposed to the irrational mind. Christians make a distinction between the *natural* mind and the *spiritual* mind.

The natural mind is not spoken of in glowing terms. It is those thought processes, inclinations, intellectual perceptions and preconceptions that reject outright any kind of data or input that might exist outside of the rational, physical realm. We've spoken earlier of naturalist thought as it relates to the cosmos (if it can't be perceived by the five senses and/or measured scientifically it doesn't exist) and the body (a strictly functional approach that snorts at biofeedback, non-medical healing, after-life experiences and the like). Natural-minded people believe that man is the measure of all things. They refuse to believe in any superior being, and insist that the answers to all our

This famous photograph, taken in 1936, shows an Indian Yogi apparently levitating, with his hand resting lightly on a cloth-draped stick. His feat was convincingly photographed from several different angles. Well-documented cases of 'impossible' feats provide tantalizing evidence that there is more to the mind and the body than we think.

deepest questions will ultimately be provided by ourselves.

The supernaturalist, on the other hand, declares that there are realms beyond those we can perceive with our physical senses. The supernaturalist is likely to believe in, or at least be sympathetic to, such phenomena as astral mind travel; astrological predictions; altered states of consciousness; biofeedback; pre- and post-existence (life before and/or after death); spiritual awareness; the power of dreams; telepathy, clairvoyance, precognition and psychokenesis . . . among other things.

Probably it would be hard to find even one thinking supernaturalist who believes in all those things with equal gusto, but you get the general idea. The supernaturalist is one who doesn't believe that what you see is necessarily all you get.

The Christian is, obviously, a supernaturalist. The Christian believes in a transcendent being — God — who brought the universe into existence, who continues to take an active part in the affairs of humanity, and who offers a plane of existence beyond this one to those who believe in him, who believe that Jesus Christ was the Son of God, and who act on those beliefs.

Jesus Christ, and those who followed him, were critical of the natural mind, and the natural way of thinking. This is because a naturalist cannot be a supernaturalist . . . naturally! A naturally-minded person cannot be a Christian. Then what is a Christian? If a Christian is, by definition, someone who believes in the supernatural, does that mean he has abandoned reason, forsaken logic? Obviously not. In fact, quite the opposite is true. Christians have a heightened sense of reality because they see the whole of reality —

SUBLIMINAL PERCEPTION

The story is now modern legend. You remember it, pilgrim: how a movie house flashed messages on the screen saying 'Eat Popcorn' and 'Drink Coca-Cola' every five seconds while the film was showing, only they did it so fast that no one in the audience actualy 'saw' the message — consciously saw it, that is. But the patrons got the message *subliminally*. It happened so fast that it slipped past normal perception, but the mind, ever-awake and greedy for stimuli, picked it right up — and popcorn sales during the interval went up 57.5 per cent; Coke sales 18 per cent.

It was supposed to have occurred in 1957, and there was quite a fuss at the time. And although a lot of people still hold with the story, subliminal seduction, as it is sometimes called, has fallen on hard times. For

a start, the incident that started the whole thing may well have been a fake. The experimenter never documented his work, and no one bothered to substantiate his claim of increased popcorn and Coke sales. Despite the lack of empirical data, lots of people were indignant anyway: civil libertarians, senators, and just about every movie-goer who had ever paid $2.00 for a medium popcorn and $1.50 for a small Coke.

But advertisers, naturally, were interested; so were eagle-eyed market researchers, account executives, film-makers and theater-owners. The lack of continued study and scientifically controlled testing allowed the subliminal perception fad to go the way of bobby sox and goldfish swallowing.

Except that now there's a psychologist named Lloyd Silverman who is using subliminal stimuli to change certain pathological conditions in his patients. And a Dr Hal Becker has come up with a little black box that he claims can plant subliminal messages in unwary shoppers: the message is broadcast right along with a store's wallpaper music, but below the threshold of normal hearing. Messages such as 'I am honest; I will not steal, it's wrong to

steal. If I steal I'll get caught', are aimed at potential thieves, in the hope that they will think twice about pocketing the merchandise. According to Becker, their 'psychostatic unconscious wishes and desires' will create an aversion to theft.

The problem in all this is that such a tool could just as well relay other urgent messages: 'Buy now! Buy lots! Charge it! Money doesn't matter! And by the way, that dress looks absolutely *fabulous* on you, darling.'

natural *and* supernatural. They work with a spiritual mind that takes the nature and activities of God into account in everything they see.

For example, the natural mind at work may look at a five-year-old child and mentally record the following data: The child is a homo sapien, an upright biped, a 32-pound mammal. It is able to perform certain tasks that are in keeping with its developmental stage: it can hop on one foot, it can ride a tricycle, it can recite the alphabet and recognize melodies. Its life expectancy is 67 years, based on data obtained from a medical history and environmental factors that influence longevity. And so on.

The supernatural mind (and more specifically, the Christian supernatural mind which recognizes a spiritual aspect to human existence) looks at the same child and notes the same data and makes similar conclusions. But it will also add that the child is the possessor of a soul, made by the Creator God for a purpose, endowed with tremendous human potential, and participating in a moral universe in which value judgments are made.

It's difficult for *anyone* to look at a five-year-old child and make only natural-minded observations. Actually, it takes a great deal of discipline to do so. For children evoke in us certain feelings that are hard to describe as attributable only to the five senses. They amuse us; they anger us; they exhaust us; they delight us; they open us to new possibilities and new ideas; they inspire us.

Taizé, a French Christian community, meets for worship. Christians believe that our inner, spiritual longings can only be fulfilled by encountering God himself.

OPTICAL ILLUSIONS

Vision is largely a process of inference. This is because the world comes to us in three dimensions, but human vision is pretty much a two-dimensional operation. The eye sees, but the brain must organize what is seen. The reliability of that organization is often questionable.

For example, this figure appears to be a set of three concentric hills with a crater-like hole in the center. The circular lines define the valleys between the ridges of hills.

But turn it over and it looks like concentric 'valleys' with a little hill in the middle. Now the circular lines define the peaks between the valleys. Try it.

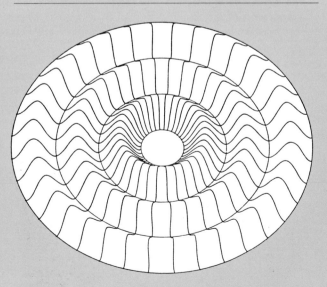

Finally, Ladies and Gentlemen, we pose the question, 'Where did it go?' by asking you if the shaded portion in this figure represents three sides of one square, or one side each of three different squares. Keep looking . . . it'll come to you. Maybe it's the way you look at it.

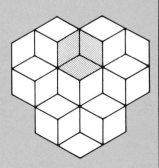

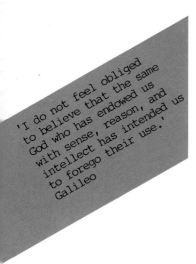

'I do not feel obliged to believe that the same God who has endowed us with sense, reason, and intellect has intended us to forego their use.'
Galileo

Now, it is true that many people today claim that they are natural thinkers. Those who observe nature are sometimes called naturalists, but this is probably a misnomer. The fact is, all protestations to the contrary, that this world has few inhabitants that work solely with their natural minds. Lucky for the world. Because the strict naturalist, in ignoring the divine, also overlooks the humanity of our species.

The contention of the *Guide* is that each individual is called upon to think both naturally and supernaturally. Each person must not only gather information, collate data, and offer conclusions (which any computer can do) but also evaluate all input and temper conclusions with the realization that there is more to this life than first meets the eye. There is also a spiritual dimension to take into account.

If Jesus and his followers were so hard on the 'natural mind' it's because purely natural thinking which denies the power of God and the preciousness of God's creation is, at its extreme, life-threatening and anti-human — two conditions absolutely abhorrent to God and right-thinking humanity.

The Apostle Paul said, 'The mind of sinful man (the natural mind) is death, but the mind controlled by the Spirit (the spiritual mind) is life and peace, because the sinful mind is hostile to God. It does not submit to God's law, nor can it do so.'

Sometimes Christians are accused of being illogical, and certainly some Christians are guilty of that charge.

But that's really beside the point, because all of humanity has an illogical streak, including those who preach logic. Since we are almost all supernaturalists, apparently by nature, we accept to some extent the assessment that not everything can be explained scientifically, rationally, logically. That there are some truly inscrutable things happening on this planet gets an 'Amen' from the human race.

Still, God is logical. He created a logical universe that runs in a profoundly logical way. There is cause and effect in the cosmos — very logical. And Jesus Christ also used logic — with great effect. He was dynamite in a debate, a skilled reasoner who could expose flaws in the logic of his opponents. Even his enemies never faulted his logic. And while there is a great deal about God and about Jesus Christ that is difficult to understand; while there are paradoxes in the Christian faith; while there are certain aspects of Jesus' teaching that are more easily understood intuitively (by the right-brain) than logically (by the left-brain), the parts that can be reasoned are absolutely reasonable.

And since the Christian believes in a life after our pilgrimage on Planet Earth, there is hope that questions not answered here may be answered at some later date. As the Bible puts it: 'For now we see through a glass, darkly: but then face to face. Now I know in part; but then shall I know even as also I am known.'

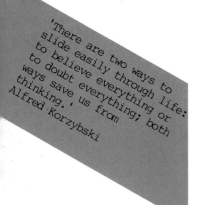

'There are two ways to slide easily through life: to believe everything or to doubt everything; both ways save us from thinking.'
Alfred Korzybski

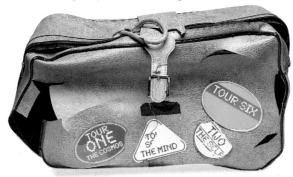

'We have probed the Earth, excavated it, burned it, ripped things from it, buried things in it... That does not fit my definition of a good tenant. If we were here on a month-to-month basis, we would have been evicted long ago.'
Rose Elizabeth Bird

The space shuttle Columbia lifts off from Cape Kennedy. Many of today's optimists have seen the limitless possibilities of space exploration as a sign of hope for the human race.

The world is obviously on the brink . . . of something.

The fact is not diminished in the least bit by another fact, which is that from time immemorial each generation has believed its world was also on the brink. The general consensus of our time, however, is that no matter what past generations may have thought, present-day events are leading up to something very important. This time the world really *is* teetering on the brink.

The United States and the Soviet Union have enough nuclear weaponry to turn both countries into glowing gravel pits many times over. The number of additional countries with nuclear capabilities continues to grow. As we turn to nuclear power to solve the problem of dwindling fossil fuel sources, we are faced with vast quantities of radioactive waste, possessing only a meager understanding of the potency of this waste, or how it may be safely contained during the millennia

required to dissipate its strength. We're on the brink of something.

The human potential movement has opened our eyes to the possibilities of the self. We see in humankind a limitless resource, heretofore untapped, a resource that can apparently address the most mind-boggling and inscrutable enigmas of human existence. As society advances, and the obstacles to fulfilment are removed, the vista of human possibilities seems limitless. We're on the brink of something.

Scientific and technological advancements are screaming ahead at break-neck speed. The scientific acquirements of the past twenty years have outdistanced the analytic achievements of all years prior. Antisepsis and antibiotics, immunizations and vaccinations, prophylaxis and anesthesia, contraception and pharmacology have lowered our birthrate and raised our life expectancy. Space-age technology has brought personal computers, satellite communication and speed-of-sound transportation into the lives of the middle class. We're on the brink of something.

Education for the masses has revolutionized our way of life. The availability of public education, the increase in world literacy and the attendant glut of information available to those who can read has expanded the horizons of the average Western person who can now move beyond the confines of tradition and establish himself in any number of areas. Unskilled workers, young children and housewives can read; they can learn; they can entertain new possibilities; they can achieve self-fulfilment. We're on the brink of something.

The doors of the global larder are swung wide open for a third of the world's population and all but closed for the rest. The Western world feasts on corn-fed beef, consumes its fill of chicken, pork and seafood, quenches its thirst with extravagant, non-nutritive beverages, enjoys the savory goodness of food well-seasoned and spiced, and eats more salt, sugar, fat and additives than is good for it. The struggling Third World countries export their succulent treasures to the West, and struggle to feed their own people. In Iowa, farmers burn their crops to protect a fair price while starvation continues year after year in North Africa as the Sahara Desert expands to consume more and more tillable land. We're on the brink of something.

The extended family passed away for much of the world a generation ago; the nuclear family that took its place is apparently unable to cope with the demands of the modern world. We search for intimacy with our fellow human beings, fighting the depersonalization of a technological society. We want to be surrounded by 'significant others', but are afraid to leave our homes at night in search of friendship. Our primary relationships are few; most of the people we are in contact with on a daily basis are mere functionaries who could just as well be efficient robots as human beings like ourselves. We're on the brink of something.

DOOMSDAY OR UTOPIA?

What do you think we're on the brink of, Pilgrim?

Perhaps you're a pessimist. You see a limited future. You have believed all along that we're on the Eve of Destruction, and now you see the dread approach of midnight as the Doomsday Clock ticks off the fatal seconds. We've gone too far, you contend. We've crested the final hill and we're teetering to the plunge.

The fossil fuels are almost gone, and nuclear power is no answer. It's just a matter of time before one of the super-powers (or some upstart nation flexing its muscles) goes berserk and pushes the button that will signal the holocaust. Or maybe it won't happen that way at all. Maybe the radioactive waste clumsily buried all over the world will start seeping out of its fragile containers, poisoning the life on earth and in the oceans, sterilizing the land as well as those who pollute it. Maybe we'll have a slow-motion annihilation.

Our scientists will continue to pursue madness, claims the pessimistic pilgrim. They will continue to ignore the human implications of their knowledge and we'll all pay for their sin. The greed of the developed world will starve the developing world: plague, famine and war will unite to solve the problem of overpopulation in the most violent way.

Humanity will be unable to adjust. There will be no transformation of the human spirit. There isn't time. Materialism will obscure reality, as we blindly continue on our self-destructive course, fiddling frantically while the world burns. And our over-educated minds will fail to comprehend the truth until it is too late.

The optimistic pilgrim says, 'Not so! It's all behind us now . . . the worst is over. There is a light at the end of the tunnel, and we're moving toward that light with the greatest speed.'

Things are not so bad, contends the optimist. The horrors of the past are over. The heart of humankind has truly softened; we've learned from our mistakes. We no longer practice wholesale cruelty on one another as we once did. There is a metaphysical evolution taking place. We are kinder; we reach out to help those in need all over the world; we claim citizenship in the global village; we no longer keep other human beings as slaves; women and children are allowed full personhood, no longer considered chattel to be bought, sold, and

An Ethiopian boy, one of millions of children affected by the North African drought and famine of the early 1980s. But famines are not caused by weather conditions alone. Powerful nations control international trade so that the poor stay poor. If we cannot solve Earth's problems, what hope is there in space exploration?

Pollution. The thinker Edward de Bono suggested that factories on rivers should have their water inlet downstream of their water outlet, and not vice versa. Polluters certainly need to be made aware of the effects of their pollution.

exploited; the Crusades and the Inquisition will never be replayed; there is unprecedented tolerance for variant points of view; we can think and reason and understand our problems and we can devise workable solutions to our dilemmas.

Fewer of our race around the world are dying prematurely from the age-old plagues of humankind. We have virtually extinguished many of the diseases that used to claim millions of lives — polio, smallpox, diphtheria. We have the medical knowledge needed to prolong our lives far beyond the expectancy of previous generations. We are taller, stronger, smarter and more able than ever.

We are no longer slaves to technology; the humanities are being taught and practiced alongside the sciences. We are, for the first time, demanding and receiving accountability from those who lead us — scientifically, politically, and socially. We have clearly seen the

mistakes of the past, and are planning our future in such a way that they will not be repeated. There has never been a better time to be alive than this time, and it's getting better with each passing day. Things are looking up for the first time in a long time.

And the vast majority of us, in an effort to stay sane, have decided that it's all we can do to just live our own lives, much less worry about the problems of the world. We do what we can to live responsibly, and comfort ourselves with the thought that somehow it'll all work out in the end: it always has, and it always will. There's no reason to assume that this generation will be the last. The world has had its problems, but always survived and this age is no different.

Now, what's for lunch?

THE NEW AGE MEETS THE KINGDOM

What's for lunch, indeed. Because the problems of living in this world can be so overwhelming that we check out completely. We are terrified to look at the big picture and instead busy ourselves with mundane matters in the hope that preoccupation with details will divert our attention from the larger issues.

Throughout this *Guide* we have been at pains to affirm all that is good in New Age thought. The *Guide* thinks that these truly are great times to be living in, and much of what is happening now in terms of philosophy, theology, politics, lifestyle, social awareness, scientific discovery and personal commitment is deserving of notice, deserving of praise. Most of us can say today that we'd rather be living right now than at any other time in history, and this in itself endorses our times.

In addition to affirming what is good in our times, we have also made it a point to show where Christian thought intersects and where it parts company with the popular movements of our day. This arises out of our conviction that the true New Age

began almost 2,000 years ago when Jesus Christ, who was God's own son, put on an Earth Suit and lived on this planet for a brief time.

Some may wonder why a 2,000-year-old religion could possibly be thought to have any relationship whatsoever to what is going on today. It's true that Christianity appears to be ancient history while the New Age looks distinctly contemporary. But the *Guide's* position is that many of the current philosophies and movements are merely playing back to us — in their own way — what Christ talked about so many years ago. In our shortsightedness, we may perceive the current emphasis on human potential, social awareness, relationship commitment, and alternate planes of existence as 20th-century thinking, when in reality they are first-century ideas. Much of it was born when Jesus Christ started talking about the Kingdom of God.

An important note from the authors: We do not wish to convey the idea that the Kingdom of God is the same thing as the New Age. This is simply not true. The New Age as popularly understood bears only a passing resemblance to the Kingdom of God in that it generally acknowledges that there is more to life than what we perceive with our five senses, more going on in the universe than what we can measure with scientific instruments, and planes of existence that are not fully known to us at this time. The New Age is not the Kingdom. But the Kingdom can be said to be New Age.

Devoted as we are to the concept of pilgrimage — embarking on a significant journey to a significant destination — and to the questioning and growth that often comes with

Waste products from nuclear fission can remain radioactive for thousands of years. The million-gallon tanks in this photograph are being built to safely contain the waste. But can such lethal matter ever be stored with complete safety?

such a journey, we can only be grateful that this is an age of flux, of change, where we find a healthy climate for growth, a desire for deeper understanding, and a willingness to discover truth.

And so it is our belief that no pilgrim can journey through the New Age without carefully scrutinizing the Christian path. There is no area of human discovery, no corner of the universe, no relationship, no fact or fantasy, no place in human consciousness that cannot and should not be explored without reference to the life and teachings of Jesus Christ. For he had something to say about all of it. The Bible, our best record of what he said and did, throws light on this age, and points the way to eternal truth.

SIGNS OF CONSCIOUS LIFE

We've mentioned several times that Christians are often caught between two apparently conflicting beliefs, and that the dynamic between these beliefs is what defines their faith. For example, there seems obvious conflict in the idea that the human soul contains an element of the divine, yet at the same time harbors a baseness that contradicts the godliness. But both are fact, and only through an appreciation of both can one arrive at the truth.

Another enigmatic belief: that humans live in Earth Suits which are, simply put, the essential equipment needed to survive a relatively brief existence on Planet Earth; nobody gets to stay even a microsecond without an Earth Suit. When the Earth Suit is worn out or destroyed, as it inevitably is, life will continue in another realm. At the same time, the no-deposit-no-return Earth Suit cannot be regarded lightly, or mistreated in any way, because it is a gift from the Creator of the

Universe, who demands conscientious caretaking of everything he has given. The Earth Suit is both priceless and expendable, all at the same time.

Jesus Christ was completely human while he lived on this earth, and also completely divine — 100 per cent man, 100 per cent God. While he ate and drank and slept and got tired and experienced every quality of humanness, he was simultaneously God: supreme, all-powerful, infinite love, wholly divine.

In the same vein, we see that Christians are necessarily optimists and pessimists concerning the state of affairs on Planet Earth. They know that this world has fallen victim to humankind's inadequacy, rebellion and cruelty, and to the evil of God's archrival, the Devil. They also know that our world is the perfect place for God's human creation to live, a custom-made environment for a custom-made people.

Does this mean that the Christian faith lacks clarity, or intellectual viability? Does the presence of so much conflicting ideology make Christianity a fool's belief?

Remember that we said previously that human beings are unique in their ability to process apparently contradictory data concurrently, and that this is the unmistakeable mark of human consciousness. The ability to deal with ambiguity, conflict, uncertainty, doubt and puzzles, is a uniquely human ability, and it is a major hallmark of our species.

Lower animals can't do it. Mark Twain said that a cat who has been burned by sitting on a hot stove will never make the mistake of sitting on a hot stove again — nor experience the pleasure of sitting on a warm one, either. The cat can only react to the world around it on an instinctual level — burned once and it's off stoves for life. So the cat's lack of rationality prevents it from putting the hot-stove-burned-bottom experience into practical perspective.

But human beings can reason; they can analyze data, figure out puzzles, project outcomes and explain phenomena. Human beings have consciousness, a dimension lacking in our animal, vegetable and mineral cohabitants.

We are not on this Earth to live an instinctual, action-reaction existence, a two-dimensional existence where all phenomena are easily explained. Our universe is three-dimensional (maybe four- or more-dimensional) and our lives reflect a multi-dimensional existence.

Some people fight this complexity, living by simple theories that they claim explain everything. And when their assumptions are challenged, they get testy. You remember how it was once believed that the universe revolved around the Earth? That was a plausible theory that appeared to explain everything . . . for a while. Most of the world wasn't willing to question it. Then along comes Copernicus, saying the Earth was not the center of all creation and all of a sudden you've got a bunch of angry people who are less interested in evaluating their beliefs in the light of hard evidence than in persecuting original thinkers. They don't want anything to challenge their neat little beliefs, not even the truth.

Others simply ignore contradiction and complexity. They just don't like to question, to explore meaning, to grapple with tough answers. They're like ostriches with their heads in the sand. 'Who can figure it?' they say, as they prepare for yet another nose dive into the beach.

The *Guide*, on the other hand, celebrates the complexity and inexplicability of life. For surely there's glory in a young man with an IQ of thirty who can play the piano as beautifully as Leslie Lemke, or who can create the exquisite drawings of Richard Wawro. The *Guide* is honored to live in a world absolutely throbbing with the mystery of love and the unsettling ambiguity of artistic expression. We are devoted to dreams, enigmas and surprises. We want to look out at night at a sky so full of stars that nobody can even begin to count them.

THE SECRET OF THE KINGDOM

The life and sayings of Jesus Christ are certainly filled with paradoxes and puzzles. He had a way of defying all conventions, upsetting the norms, saying the most scandalous things, and confusing those who thought they just might have him figured out.

Many times, Jesus conveyed his message in the form of metaphors, and through the use of fiction spoke the truths of the Kingdom of God. Metaphor, you will remember, is the language of consciousness. Only the conscious mind can utilize it. This sort of cryptic intricacy infuriated those who wanted easy answers, a cut-and-dried Grand Unifying Theory that would sew up their world into a nice, compact, portable package. But it was Christ's way to shun simple, tidy little answers. He revealed the secrets of his Kingdom by provoking his followers, teasing their interest, presenting them with just a glimpse of the magnitude of God, revealed in parables.

Some people thought that when Jesus Christ spoke of the Kingdom of God he was talking about a political system that would overthrow the corrupt Roman empire that was oppressing so many of the people. Similarly, many people think of the New Age today in terms of political revolution, or at least political reform.

Others thought that the Kingdom of God was a pie-in-the-sky-by-and-by sort of affair. They believed that the world was already kaput, so their only hope was in a bright hereafter where things just had to be better. 'It's no use,' they said. 'Why bother trying to

change things in the here and now?' Some New Agers today feel the same way. They've all but abandoned the physical world in search of alternate realities, cosmic consciousness, and higher planes of existence.

But Christ said that the Kingdom of God was neither — not a political panacea, not a cosmic never-never land. What he did say about it is riddled with ironies. He said that the Kingdom of God itself (the *true* New Age) was not of this world, and yet that it was 'at hand' — that is, already happening. He said if someone wanted to be really great in the Kingdom, he should concentrate on being a servant. Asked for an example of greatness, he pointed to a little child. He referred to himself both as the Son of God and the Son of Man.

The most breathtaking claim of all, and the most puzzling, was that in Jesus the Kingdom had actually come. He was announcing a New Age in which wrong would be put right, sin and evil would be no more, the sick would be healed, the prisoners released, righteousness and social justice would replace the injustice and inhumanity of man against man . . .

But how could this be? Jesus proclaimed it, demonstrated it in his power over nature, sickness, even death. But then he himself seemed to fall victim to the injustice and

violence and scheming sinfulness of the old order. He died as an agitator, as a blasphemer who claimed to be God.

But after three days dead and buried, Jesus became alive again. His body was still a body. He ate and drank (and ghosts don't do that). But his body was different, as if different energy laws were at work. He came and went — he was seen by thousands. Finally he left his followers with a commission: to announce to the world that in him, in Jesus, others too could share the life of the Kingdom, the real New Age. He had died the death once for all the sin and violence and corruption of the Old Order. He had demonstrated in his victory over death and new life that the New Order had begun — and others could share it as they shared in him.

So today we live in the overlap of the ages, waiting for the Old Order to be finally wound up and the New Order to be completely revealed. The old creation is in its death pangs. The new creation shows its birth pangs in the new people who are the forerunners of a time when all things shall be made new.

KINGDOM LIVING

How does possessing citizenship in God's kingdom affect your life? On the surface it looks pretty confusing. We must obviously grapple with the flesh-and-blood issues of everyday living, yet recognize our existence as spiritual beings. Can it happen?

The here-and-now is important. Christ gave no encouragement for dropping out of society, shunning our fellow travelers, or getting so strung out on soul trips that we lose touch with reality.

Jesus himself is our best example of how the Christian life should be lived: always concerned with human problems and situations, but aware that God is the ultimate answer to the

'The kingdom of heaven is like this. A man is looking for fine pearls, and when he finds one that is unusually fine, he goes out and sells everything he has, and buys that pearl.'
Jesus Christ

'A man prayed, and at first he thought that prayer was talking. But he became more and more quiet until in the end he realized that prayer is listening' Soren Kierkegaard. *At the heart of the Christian experience is the living God, reaching out to communicate with us.*

human dilemma. Our job is to live life. Jesus said that the reason he came at all was so that we would have true life, abundant life. Life is what we're here for; it's important. And every now and then, those of us who claim citizenship in the Kingdom will get a small taste of what the future will be like: we get it every time we practice justice, peace, mercy, freedom, love and brotherhood, forgiveness and joy.

Jesus shows us that we have been created to use our minds, to exercise our creativity, to enjoy the beauty around us, to take good care of our Earth Suits, to watch out for our planet, to establish relationships centered in God, to help those in need, to fight for justice, to conduct ourselves while on this pilgrimage as faithful children of a heavenly father, and to point our fellow travelers toward the truth.

THE KINGDOM LIVES

People haven't changed much in the past 2,000 years. We're still caught up in our drive to achieve, our commitment to ourselves, our fear of the unknown, our struggle for understanding. The words of Jesus still speak to us today, and call us out of our self-made world, our petty concerns, our short-sighted vision. The message of Jesus continues to set people free.

There are always some who aren't interested in the upside-down Kingdom. It doesn't make sense to them. They're devoted to the idea that, given time, they can figure out the mysteries of life on their own. Or they're such convinced humanists, believing that humankind itself holds the answer to all of humankind's problems, that they can't see any other way. Or they're simply too proud to accept the fact that they are needy, rebellious creatures who could make good use of the kind of help that only God can give. They cannot bring themselves to confess any inadequacy, or admit to any wrongdoing, any sin.

But there are also those today who respond to the teachings of Jesus. They know that their attempts at solving their own problems, of looking to themselves for the answers to life's questions, have been one miserable failure after another. Their fragile theories continually shatter in the wake of new experiences and new evidence. They can't make sense of the world they live in; they can't find their place. They know that money, knowledge, relationships, self-indulgence and self-actualization haven't brought them happiness or peace of mind. They suspect there is more to life and feel as if they're missing something.

They respond to the love of God that was perfectly expressed when Jesus came to live on this earth. They appreciate the sacrifice that Jesus made when he — Creator of the Universe — put on an Earth Suit and came and lived here as a human being just as we are required to do. These people admit that they have failed, that their pride and selfishness and sin stand between them and God; they want to be rid of everything that keeps them from being close to God. Painful as it is, they would rather admit inadequacy and change than continue to live in darkness and ignorance.

They are ready to leave the old ways behind, ready to start living in the Kingdom of God.

Now, it's not up to you or me or any other pilgrim to concoct the Kingdom. A lot of people in the past have become really excited about creating a Utopia, but history shows that it has never worked. Humankind has not yet been able to establish heaven on earth, and it never will, because it's plainly impossible. Furthermore, it's not our job. Our job is to look for the Kingdom of God and, having found it, to enter into it. You look, you find, you live.

For the Kingdom of God represents God's active reign in the world — right here and now, on Planet Earth. Whenever God's will is being done in an individual's life and in the events of history, whenever we are willing to be subjects of the head of the Kingdom (God), then the Kingdom is revealed. In Jesus Christ, the Kingdom has become a reality. God's rule is happening. And the future will show the ultimate expression of the Kingdom.

Each one of us, regardless of who we are, what we have done, where we live, or in what epoch we live, can become a part of the Kingdom by believing in Christ, believing that he is the Son of God, that he loves us enough to save us from evil, from ourselves and our rebelliousness. We believe, and then resolve to live a life that reflects our belief.

And when this part of our life is
over, the part that takes place on
Planet Earth, we can count on a new
kind of life — a multi-dimensional,

technicolor kind of life where justice,
mercy, beauty, peace and freedom are
not the exception, but the rule.

If you have enjoyed your trip through the New Age, don't miss the others: *Pilgrim's Guide to the Future*, and *Pilgrim's Guide to the Past*.